MW01592279

Frederic Chopin; his life, letters, and works Volume v.1

Karasowski, Maurycy, 1823-1892, Hill, Emily

Nabu Public Domain Reprints:

You are holding a reproduction of an original work published before 1923 that is in the public domain in the United States of America, and possibly other countries. You may freely copy and distribute this work as no entity (individual or corporate) has a copyright on the body of the work. This book may contain prior copyright references, and library stamps (as most of these works were scanned from library copies). These have been scanned and retained as part of the historical artifact.

This book may have occasional imperfections such as missing or blurred pages, poor pictures, errant marks, etc. that were either part of the original artifact, or were introduced by the scanning process. We believe this work is culturally important, and despite the imperfections, have elected to bring it back into print as part of our continuing commitment to the preservation of printed works worldwide. We appreciate your understanding of the imperfections in the preservation process, and hope you enjoy this valuable book.

FREDERIC CHOPIN

HIS LIFE, LETTERS, AND WORKS

BY

MORITZ KARASOWSKI.

With Portrait.

TRANSLATED FROM THE GERMAN BY

EMILY HILL.

" Chopin is and remains the boldest and proudest poetic spirit of the age."—
ROBERT SCHUMANN

IN TWO VOLUMES.—VOL. I.

LONDON:

WILLIAM REEVES, 185, FLEET STREET,
Publisher of Musical Works.

1879.

19720

G. HILL, STEAM PRINTER,

WESTMINSTER BRIDGE ROAD,

LONDON.

Music Library
ML

CONTENTS.

CONTENTS.

To HERMANN SCHOLTZ.

Our frequent conversations on Chopin have taught me to respect you as an admirer of this great master, and as a true and faithful interpreter of his glorious productions. It is to you, therefore, that I dedicate this work, which, without vanity, I may call a monument raised with care and devotion to his memory.

Accept it as a proof of my sincere friendship and appreciative esteem for your talents.

MORITZ KARASOWSKI.

Dresden, January, 1877.

PREFACE.

SEVERAL years of friendship with the family of
Frederic Chopin have enabled me to become acquainted with his letters and to place them before
the public. Just as I had finished transcribing the
first series (letters of his youth) and was on the point
of chronologically arranging the second (Paris correspondence) the insurrection of 1863 broke out in
Poland, and the sympathy aroused by the political
condition of the Fatherland weakened public interest
in its literary and artistic productions. I therefore
deemed it advisable to abstain from the publication
of Chopin's letters.

When I gave back to his family the original
letters, I did not dream that in a few months they
would be destroyed. How this happened I shall
in the proper place explain. The loss is a great
and irreparable one, for the number of letters from
Paris, during a most brilliant and interesting epoch,
was by no means inconsiderable.

In compliance with the wishes of many of Chopin's

friends and admirers, I have undertaken to sketch his career from the materials afforded me by his one surviving sister, from his letters which I published in Warsaw, and from some other letters to his friends.

In this work, which contains full particulars about Chopin's youth, I have corrected the erroneous dates and mis-statements, which have found their way into all the German and French periodicals and books. If I should succeed in presenting the reader with a life-like portrait of the immortal artist, it will be the highest reward of my labour of love.

THE AUTHOR.

LIFE OF CHOPIN.

CHAPTER I.

NICHOLAS CHOPIN'S FAMILY AND FRIENDS.
ZYWNY. ELSNER.

IN the year 1787 Warsaw was in a state of
unwonted excitement, for the thoughts of the
people were attracted to and concentrated upon
the Diet, that was shortly to assemble for the
purpose of preserving the Polish nation from the
miseries incident to anarchy, for upholding the
Republic, remodelling old and defective laws, and
framing new ones in harmony with the requirements of the times.

A radical reform of the effete Constitution was
considered by high State functionaries, the clergy,
and by the old nobility, to be necessary. Admittedly,

A

the Republic ought to be strong enough to protect
itself against hostile foreign influence, or a repetition
of the dismemberment of 1773. Consequently, an
imposing standing army was organized, and, for the
purpose of raising the *status* of the citizens, special
privileges were granted to the trading classes, and
the serfs were emancipated. Indeed, the patriots
were desirous of making all classes politically equal.

The election of members for the Diet was conducted in a spirit of true patriotic zeal, and nearly
all classes in Warsaw were taking part in the necessary arrangements. Many of the noblest families
removed to the capital. Foreign ambassadors attended the palace to ascertain the intentions of King
Stanislas Augustus respecting the thorough reforms
required by the people. The chariots of the highest
official functionaries, Wojewoden, and Kastellane,
frequently accompanied by outriders in their gorgeous national costume, and carriages, filled with
elegantly dressed ladies, rolled along the streets;
while everywhere there prevailed a bustle and excitement long unknown in Warsaw.

The whole nation was inspired by the hope of a
brighter future. The nobility were to aid a peaceful
revolution by voluntarily renouncing their privileges
in favour of a younger generation. The future Republic was viewed in the most glowing light. Notwithstanding the recent partition which had rent the
very heart of the country, and narrowly circumscribed
its boundaries, every patriot believed that Poland

would now rise from the degradation caused by long years of anarchy, and, strengthened with new energy, defy every danger.

No wonder the inhabitants of the capital witnessed the preparations for the important Diet with enthusiasm, or that the streets were thronged with people. Members of the aristocracy, famous for their patriotism and willing self-sacrifice for the good both of the people and the Republic, were universally greeted with genuine esteem and affection. Such was the scene of stirring activity presented by the capital during the preparations for the quadrennial Diet.

Among the crowds which thronged the chief thoroughfares was a young Frenchman, just arrived from his own country. Everything that met his eye—from the dress of the burgher to the gorgeous apparel of the rich noble, who at that time generally wore the picturesque national costume—fixed his attention, and appeared to him unusually interesting and original. This stranger was Nicholas Chopin, father of the renowned pianist and tone-poet.

Nicholas Chopin was born at Nancy, in Lorraine, April 17th, 1770. The duchies of Lorraine and Bar passed, as is well-known, by the peace of Vienna, in 1735, into the possession of the King of Poland, Stanislas Leszczynski, after whose death they reverted to France.

Stanislas Leszczynski, a constant friend to science and art, made great efforts for the spread of general culture among his people ; he founded, at Nancy, the

still-existing "Academie Stanislai," and by his just
and mild rule won the undivided esteem and affection
of his subjects. Nicholas Chopin was born when the
remembrance of this prince and philosopher was still
in its first freshness. It had long been the desire of
Chopin, and many other educated Lorrainers, who
knew something of the history of Poland, to visit the
country of the exiled monarch who ruled their own
little land, and to become acquainted with a nation
which, despite its own needs, was ever ready to
assist the wants of others.

An opportunity soon presented itself. The Starostin
Lacynska, who met Nicholas Chopin, at Nancy,
and was prepossessed by his highly cultured mind
and amiable manners, offered him the appointment
of tutor to her two children, which he readily accepted. Bidding adieu to his family and friends,
he followed the Starostin, and arrived in Warsaw
during the political agitation of 1787.

During his residence with Starostin Lacynska, in
the city, and at the village of Czerniejow, the young
Frenchman became acquainted with many important
official personages, some of whom played a prominent part in the Diet.

He early perceived that a study of the manners
and customs of the people required a thorough
knowledge of the language, and in that acquisition
he soon made considerable progress. The dis-
cussions in the Diet interested him much, because
they revealed the many wrongs inflicted on a nation

which, under the sceptre of the Jagiellons, had been among the most powerful and distinguished.

Nicholas Chopin, also, witnessed some important political celebrations in Warsaw. The proclamation of the new Constitution of the 3rd May, 1791, made a deep and permanent impression upon him.*

With the exception of a few obstinately prejudiced aristocrats, the results of the Diet were received by the whole nation with unexampled enthusiasm. The joy of the people of Warsaw was unbounded, and everyone hoped for a return of the golden age of Poland, as the reign of Sigismund August II. has been rightly called.

As Nicholas Chopin found his social pleasures exclusively among Polish circles, he began to regard Poland as his second home, and heartily sympathised with the memorable act which promised brighter fortunes to the land of the Sarmatians. The recollection of this period never faded from his memory, and he would often describe to his family the transport and enthusiasm of the people who thought its future happiness assured by a firm government, the equality of all classes before the law, and a standing army of 100,000 men.

---

* Speaking of this new Constitution, Fox said, " It is a work, in which every friend to reasonable liberty must be sincerely interested." Burke exclaimed: " Humanity must rejoice and glory when it considers the change in Poland."— *Translator's Note.*

Unfortunately these bright hopes were but short lived. Jealous neighbours, to whose interests the re-organization and strengthening of Poland were inimical, foreswore its downfall. Contrary to all principles of justice, for Poland had not in the smallest degree meddled in her affairs, Russia was the first to take up arms, under the pretext of opposing the Jacobite tenets of the Constitution and of restoring to the nobles the power taken from them by the people. The lust of power and the corruptibility of certain magnates were used by the Russian government for its own iniquitous ends, and the good laws decreed by the quadrennial Diet never came into operation.

Frederick William II.,* of Prussia—although he professed friendship for Poland, praised the Constitution, and on March 29th, 1790, concluded, through his ambassador in Warsaw, Lucchesini, an offensive and defensive alliance, guaranteeing the national independence—did not hesitate to enter into a mutual engagement with Russia for a second partition of Poland, by which he received, in the year 1793, an area of 1,100 square miles, in the neighbourhood of Dantzic and Thorn. From this time until its total

---

* In a letter to the King of Poland, dated May 23rd, he said, " I congratulate myself on having had it in my power to maintain the liberty and independence of the Polish nation, and one of my most pleasing cares will be to support and draw closer the bond which unites us."—*Translator's Note.*

annihilation, one misfortune after another beset the sorely tried nation. When the weak and vacillating King Stanislas Augustus not only deserted his people, because they defended their independence and the Constitution of May 3rd, but even joined the Russian party, the great Polish families, one by one, left Warsaw for more secure abodes.

Nicholas Chopin, having lost his appointment with Starostin Laczynska, resolved to leave the country; illness, however, forced him to remain in Warsaw. He, therefore, witnessed, in 1794, the revolution of which Kosciuszko was the hero, and also the siege of the capital by the Prussians. Brave by nature, and zealous for the independence of Poland, Nicholas Chopin entered the ranks of the National Guards, and took an active part in the defence of the country. He had attained the position of captain at the time of the defeat of the Polish army at Maciejowice, when Kosciuszko was severely wounded and taken prisoner, and overwhelming forces were marching on the suburb of Praga. Nicholas Chopin was ordered thither with his company, and his death would have been inevitable had he not been relieved from his post by another company a few hours before the occupation.

It is notorious that, after the capture of Praga, November 5th, 1794, Suwarow ordered his troops to kill all the inhabitants, old men, women, and children not excepted. More than 10,000 persons fell victims to the conqueror's cruelty. The third

partition of Poland, which was accomplished in the
following year, gave the death blow to its political
existence. Poland disappeared from the ranks of
nations, and figured only on the map of Europe in
fragments, incorporated with other States. Warsaw
alone was under Prussian supremacy.

After passing through this stormy period, Nicholas
Chopin once more resolved to return to France ; but
was again seized by a severe illness, which forbade
him undergoing the fatigue and delay which the
long journey at that time involved. He, therefore,
remained in Warsaw, and supported himself by
giving lessons in French. When asked why he
had abandoned the idea of returning to his own
country, he used to reply : " I have twice made the
attempt, but was prevented both times by a severe
illness, which almost cost me my life ; it seems to
be the will of Providence that I should stay in
Poland, and I willingly submit."

In the beginning of the present century we find
Nicholas Chopin established in the house of the
Countess Skarbek, as tutor to her son. He there
met and fell in love with Fräulein Justine Krzyza-
nowska, whom, in 1806, he married. Their union
was blessed with three daughters and one son.
Count Frederic Skarbek was god-father to the latter,
and gave him his own baptismal name, " Frederic."

While little Frederic's parents were rejoicing in
his growth and development, the political condition
of Poland again changed. The formation of the

Grand Duchy of Warsaw, by Napoleon I., in the year 1807, on the basis of the peace of Tilsit, aroused the Poles from the political death sleep into which they had sunk after the last partition of their country. Raised by the successful conqueror to the importance of an actual capital, Warsaw became the centre of action, animating and concentrating all the powers of the newly-made Duchy. Thither everyone eagerly repaired. With impetuous haste a government was organized, a soldiery formed, and new schools established. Following the general example, Nicholas Chopin returned with his family to Warsaw, where he would be able to work with greater advantage both to himself and to the country of his adoption. On October 1st, 1810, he was appointed Professor of French at the newly established Lyceum, where he continued in active work for twenty-one years, that is, until its overthrow by the Russian government. On January 1st, 1812, he entered on similar duties at the School of Artillery and Engineering.

When the kingdom of Poland had been restored, on the basis of the Congress of Vienna, principally out of those portions which had previously formed the Grand Duchies, Nicholas Chopin undertook the professorship of French at the Military Elementary School. The insurrection of November 29th, 1830, which had awakened among Polish patriots hopes of deliverance from Russian domination, ended in total discomfiture.

Fresh misfortunes visited the country. The most intelligent portion of the nation and the representatives of the government emigrated, the army was disbanded, the universities removed, the Lyceum and other educational establishments closed. Nicholas Chopin was a member of the Examining Committee for candidates for appointments in the public schools, and finally became professor at the Academy for Roman Catholic Clergy.

The strenuous exertions undertaken by Chopin, out of love for his adopted country, induced a gradual failure of his powers; he, therefore, accepted a pension, and retired from public life. His integrity and noble-mindedness, his dignity under adverse fortune, and the blameless purity of his life, caused him to be highly respected in the country he had made his own. The best Polish families were anxious to entrust the training of their sons to his care, and to place them in a household universally esteemed, so that for some years Nicholas Chopin had the charge of a considerable number of youths who were educated with his own son Frederic. Anxiety about his son did much to becloud the last years of his life. Amid the devoted care of his family Nicholas Chopin died, in 1844, aged seventy-four.

Justine Chopin, who had shared all her husband's joys and troubles, was of an exceedingly gentle disposition, and excelled in all womanly virtues. The fame of her son Frederic, did not render her in the least haughty. Domestic peace was her highest

happiness.   Providence afflicted her with severe
trials : after the death of her husband she lost two
amiable daughters, and then her only and dearly
loved son, the last moments of whose life she was
unable to soothe by her motherly care.   But these
afflictions were borne with touching patience.   In
extreme old age she lived in the house of her one
surviving daughter; her last days were devoted
almost entirely to prayer, and she never went out
except to church.   She died October 1st, 1861.

Louisa, the eldest child, born April 6th, 1807,
received a very careful education, and soon became
a great help to her parents.   She was distinguished
by unusual intellectual gifts, industry, and very
agreeable manners.   In conjunction with her sister,
Isabella, she wrote some books on the best means
for the elevation of the working classes.   After her
marriage with Professor Jedrzejewicz, in 1832, she
devoted herself to the education of her children, and
gave less attention to literature.   She did not, however, entirely lay aside her pen, but wrote and
published, in various journals, papers and articles
on the education of youth.   She died October 29th,
1855.

Nicholas Chopin's second daughter, Isabella,
married the Inspector of Schools, Anton Barcinski,
who afterwards became Director of Steamboats.
They are both still living in Warsaw.

Emily, the youngest daughter, a very attractive
girl, of whom the highest hopes were entertained,

died in her fourteenth year, April 10th, 1827.
Educated beyond her years, unceasingly bright and
witty, she possessed the happy gift of always diffusing cheerfulness. She was, therefore, much beloved,
and her wit, affectionate flattery, or droll mimicry,
often prevailed with her parents when her elder
sisters' and even her brother's influence had been of
no avail.

Thirsting for knowledge, she worked untiringly.
The writings of the principal Polish authors, such
as Clementine and Tanska, had so deeply impressed her, that she made it the aim of her
life to become an authoress. She, therefore,
at an early age, zealously studied her mother
tongue, which she soon succeeded in mastering.
Some poems which she wrote for special occasions
were distinguished by blameless form and harmony ;
even in her thirteenth year Emily and her sister
Isabella were engaged in translating into Polish the
tales of the German writer, Salzmann ; but her
early death, unfortunately, prevented the completion
of this work. Judging from such of her poetical
effusions as still remain, it may be assumed, that
had she lived, Emily would have attained as brilliant a position in Polish literature as her brother
has in music. She suffered from an incurable com-
plaint of the chest, and, in her last moments, seeing
the suffering and despair of the relatives around her,
she repeated the lines :

"Wie bitter ist des Menschen Loos auf Erden,
  Sieht er wie um *sein* Leid, die *Seinen* traurig werden."

Thus, at the early age of fourteen, passed away this talented girl, whose premature intellectual development was so remarkable.

In contemplating the family of Frederic Chopin we see his own character in its fairest light, and understand how he became what he was. In a certain sense a human being resembles a plant: nationality, parents, family, friends, and teachers, all have a share in his development. Happy the man who regards his parents with loving reverence, who rejoices in good brothers and sisters and excellent teachers.

One of Nicholas Chopin's oldest friends was his colleague and superior, the famous philologist, Dr. Samuel Bogumil von Linde, who earned the thanks of the whole nation by the compilation of his valuable Polish dictionary. His merit is so much the greater as, independently of the labours of Wilhelm von Humboldt and Bopp, he applied the comparative and historical method to his work, thus rendering it, to speak accurately, a parallel comparison of the Slavonic languages.

Frederic Chopin often played duets with Madame von Linde, who was an unusually well educated woman, and a remarkable pianist for her time. To her Chopin dedicated his first published work, Rondo, op. 1. This composition was the first

instalment of the rare treasures with which he
has enriched the literature of music.

Another of Nicholas Chopin's colleagues was
Waclaw Alexander Maciejowski, celebrated for his
researches in history and Slavonic law. His works
are much valued by students, and have been translated into several languages.

Among others who were from time to time
Nicholas Chopin's guests were : Count Skarbek,
an excellent author, foster-son to Nicholas, and
god-father to Frederic Chopin ; the Professors of
the University, Brodzinski, poet and student of
aesthetics ; Julius Kolberg, an engineer, father of
the ethnologist Oskar, the indefatigable collector
of folk songs; Jarocki, a learned zoologist ; Anton
Brodowski, a celebrated historical and portrait
painter ; Anton Barcinski, Professor at the Poly-
technic school since 1823, teacher in the host's
pension, and afterwards his son-in-law ; Jawurek, a
talented musician ; and last of all Chopin's two
masters, Zywny and Elsner.

Adalbert Zywny, born in Bohemia, in 1756, came
to Poland in the reign of Stanislas Augustus.
His first appointment was that of music teacher
in the house of Prince Casimir Sapiecha; then he
settled in Warsaw as teacher of the piano. He
died in 1840.

Of Elsner I must speak more particularly, because, as Chopin's master for counterpoint, he first
discovered his pupil's creative originality, and by

guidance and counsel assisted considerably in the development of his talent for composition. Frederic, therefore, not only loved and valued Elsner as a teacher, but also as an intimate friend. As will be seen, his name frequently occurs in Chopin's letters. In Germany Elsner is almost unknown as a composer, although he rendered good service to church music.

Joseph Xaver Elsner was born June 29th, 1769, at Grottkau, in Silesia. His father, who was an instrument maker, wished him to study medicine, but Joseph preferred to devote himself to music. Maar, band-master at Breslau, gave him his first instruction in counterpoint. In 1792, Elsner went to Poland, holding the post of band-master and composer at the National Theatre, first at Lemberg and then in Warsaw. In 1816, after the proclamation of the institution of the new kingdom by the Congress of Vienna, he was entrusted with the establishment of a school for organists, and six years after with the direction of the Conservatoire.

Besides the German operas, " Die Seltenen Brüder," " Der Verkleidete Sultan," and " Il Flauto Magico," which Elsner composed at Lemberg, he wrote twenty-seven Polish operas and melodramas, a great number of arias, cantatas, string quartets, and three symphonies, besides several ecclesiastical works, among which the oratorio, " Das Leiden Christi " was several times performed in Warsaw, and very favourably received. Its wealth of melody, no less than its technical working, renders this one

of the chief, and, perhaps, the most successful of
Elsner's compositions.   He also rendered great
services to Poland, as teacher and director at the
Conservatoire.   He trained a considerable number
of talented young men, who afterwards became
excellent musicians, and otherwise promoted the
cultivation of music in the noblest manner.   He
died April 18th, 1854.

A magnificent monument, raised by public sub-
scription, adorns his tomb in Warsaw.

Titled landowners were also included in the circle
of Nicholas Chopin's friends.   Most of them had
been his pupils, or had become acquainted with him
through their sons.   In later years, when Frederic's
rare and brilliant talents were more fully developed,
his father counted among his guests not only *savants*,
poets, and artists, but the *élite* of the aristocracy,
who considered it an honour to become acquainted
with this interesting and highly esteemed family,
and delighted in admiring the young artist for whom
a glorious future was already prophesied.   These
were bright and happy days passed by Chopin in
his father's house.

CHAPTER II.

FREDERIC'S CHILDHOOD. HIS FIRST
APPEARANCE IN PUBLIC.
IMPROVISATIONS. POLISH NATIONAL SONGS.

ON March 1st, 1809, Frederic François Chopin was born, at Zelazowa Wola, a village six miles from Warsaw, belonging to Count Skarbek, in whose house Nicholas Chopin was tutor.*

In his earliest years Frederic was so very sensitive to music that he wept whenever he heard it, and was with difficulty restrained. This powerful influence was not a painful one; for Frederic soon showed such a decided love for the piano, that his parents obtained instruction for him, selecting as his master the well-known and excellent teacher, Albert Zywny, of Warsaw. As Frederic was so young, his elder sister shared the music lessons.

Zywny was the first and only director of Frederic's precocious musical talents, for the child began to

---

* All the foreign biographers of Chopin have mistaken the date of his birth. Even on his monument at Père la Chaise, in Paris, 1810 is engraven instead of 1809, an error which ought to have been rectified long ago.

compose before he even knew how to commit his ideas to paper. He would request his master to write down what he improvised, and these first thoughts were afterwards frequently altered and improved by the gifted boy.

Thus early did he indicate his future care in composition, and his truly artistic nature. In a few years Frederic made such progress in pianoforte playing as to excite wonder in all Warsaw drawing rooms. On the occasion of a public concert, for the benefit of the poor, February 24th, 1818, Julius Ursin Miemcewicz, late adjutant to Kosciuszko, and himself a great statesman, poet, historian, and political writer, and other high personages, invited the co-operation of the virtuoso, who had not quite completed his ninth year. Such a request could not be refused, and thus Chopin's first step in his artistic career was for a charitable object. A few hours before the performance (he was to play Gyrowetz's pianoforte Concerto), "Fritzchen," as he was called at home, was placed on a chair to be suitably dressed for his first appearance before a large assembly. The child was delighted with his jacket, and especially with the handsome collar. After the concert, his mother, who had not been present, asked, as she embraced him, "what did the public like best?" He naïvely answered: "Oh, mamma, everybody looked only at my collar," thus showing that he was not vain of his playing.

From that evening the flower of the aristocracy vied with each other in patronizing the marvellous boy, whom they regarded as an ornament of their *salons*. We merely mention the Princes Czartoryski, Sapiecha, Czetwertynski, Lubecki, Radziwill, Counts Skarbek, Wolicki, Pruszak, Hussarzewski, Lempicki. The Princess Czetwertynski introduced him to the Princess Lowicka, the unhappy wife of the Grand Prince Constantin Pawlowicz. Young, bewitchingly beautiful, full of intelligence and grace, her charms won the affections of the Grand Prince, who shunned no sacrifice to make her his own. His passion for this beautiful woman only temporarily modified his harshness and violence, and, in her wretched life, the enjoyment of art was her one solace.

Accustomed in his father's house to good society, and now having the *entrée* of the first *salons* in the capital, refined surroundings became to Frederic a second nature, and gave him the life-long impress of a gentleman. He always had an aversion to coarse people, and avoided anyone who lacked good manners.

Catalini, when passing through Warsaw, became acquainted with the youthful virtuoso, and was delighted with his artistic pianoforte playing. As a grateful recognition of the enjoyment he had afforded her, she presented him with a gold watch, on the back of which was inscribed: "Donné par Madame Catalini à Frédéric Chopin, agé de dix ans." Frederic's earliest compositions were dances,

Polonaises, Mazurkas, Waltzes; then he accomplished a March, which he ventured to dedicate to the Grand Prince Constantine. This violent man, the terror of those around him, was often very kind to the little artist; he accepted the dedication very graciously, and desired Frederic to play the piece to him. Fortunately for the young composer the Prince liked it, and he walked up and down while it was being played, smiling and beating time with the utmost complacency. He had the March * scored, and it was often performed at the military parade, in the Saxon Square.

Frederic occasionally improvised in the drawing room of the Grand Princess. Noticing his habit of casting up his eyes and gazing at the ceiling, the Prince said to him: " Why do you always look upwards, boy? do you see notes up there? " Probably Chopin saw nothing around him when listening to the voice of his genius.

From contemporary observers we learn with what perseverance he laboured to overcome the technical difficulties of the pianoforte. Impressed by the good effect of a chord with the dominant in the higher octave, but unable to play it with his small hand, he endeavoured to produce the desired expansion by a mechanical contrivance of his own manufacture, which he kept between his fingers even during the

---

* This March was afterwards published in Warsaw, but without the composer's name.

night.   He was not led to use this aid by a desire of
fame or of forestalling others, in inventing and sur-
mounting new difficulties, but because he perceived
the difference between a slurred and a detached
chord.   These chords became a characteristic feature
in Chopin's compositions.   At first they were thought
almost impossible for systematic use, but players
grew accustomed to them, and now no pianist finds
them unsuited to the capacities of the hand.

The refinement and elegance of Chopin's musical
ideas, and his obvious desire for the frequent use of
extended chords, already reveal his peculiar *penchant*
for new, dissevered chords.   Perceiving Frederic's
uncommon talent for composition, his father had
him instructed in counterpoint, as far as was com-
patible with his preparation for the Warsaw Lyceum,
not having as yet entertained the idea of making
him an artist.   Nicholas Chopin made a most
fortunate choice in asking his friend, Elsner, to
become Frederic's instructor.   Teacher and pupil
were united till death, in a pure and faithful friendship, such as only the noblest minds can feel.
When people remarked to Elsner, as they frequently
did, that Frederic under-rated and set aside the
customary rules and universal laws of music, and
listened only to the dictates of his own fancy, the
worthy director of the Conservatoire would reply :
" Leave him alone, he does not follow the common
way because his talents are uncommon ; he does not
adhere to the old method because he has one of his

own, and his works will reveal an originality hitherto unknown." This prophecy has been fully fulfilled. A less discerning teacher might have hindered and repressed his pupil's efforts, and so quenched the desire for loftier flights. To the astonishment of his friends, Frederic excelled in everything he undertook, and they formed the most brilliant expectations of his future. Extraordinary vivacity of temperament prompted him to incessant activity, and sharpened his innate, irrepressible, and versatile humour. What innumerable tricks he was continually playing on his sisters, schoolfellows, and even on persons of riper years! His youngest sister, Emily, was an active assistant in these merry pranks.

The birthdays of his parents and intimate friends were frequently celebrated by theatrical representations, in which Frederic usually took the most active part. The eminent dramatic artist of that time, Albert Piasecki, who acted as manager at these representations, considered that Chopin, on account of his presence of mind, excellent declamation, and capacity for rapid facial changes, was born to be a great actor. Frederic's acting, indeed, often astonished the best connoisseurs. He frequently saved a piece by improvising his own and other parts, when one of the players forgot his *rôle*, or the prompter failed to assist. It is well known that his talent for musical improvisation contributed in no small degree in after years to his fame.

Having, under the excellent guidance of Elsner,
mastered the technicalities of music, Chopin could
improvise to an unlimited extent on any given
theme, producing the most graceful changes, and
drawing the most marvellous effects from the key-
board. In these improvisations, and particularly
in those of a later period, Chopin showed himself
a true poet, and this explains why poets admired
him so ardently and felt inspired by his playing.
Those who heard Chopin at such times say that
his finest compositions are but a reflex and echo
of his improvisations. When Frederic was fifteen,
and Emily eleven, they wrote in honour of their
father's birthday, a one-act comedy, in verse, entitled: "The Mistake; or, the Imaginary Rogue."
Frederic, Isabella, and Emily took the principal
parts, the others were divided among the boarders.
The comedy is too ephemeral and naïve for quota-
tion, but it displayed the intelligence of the youthful
authors, and their command of language. In the
same year (1824) Frederic entered the fourth class
at the Lyceum, and although he frequently indulged
in his harmless and always witty pranks, he was
one of the best and most talented pupils. He used
to make his fellow students laugh by caricaturing the
professor of history discoursing on great celebrities.
In a lucky moment, he caricatured the director,
Mons. Linde, to the life, but unfortunately the drawing fell into the director's hands. This worthy man,
who was indulgent to everyone, and especially to the

young, returned the paper to Chopin, without a
word, having written on it, "the likeness is well
drawn." For a long time Frederic took a delight in
catching the ludicrous side of a characteristic figure,
and caricaturing it.

He spent his first holidays in Mazovia, at the
village of Szafarnia, which belonged to the Dziewa-
nowski estate, where he soon formed a warm and
lasting friendship with the children of this distinguished family. To any boy brought up in a
city, a stay of several weeks in the country is a
time full of freedom and delight ; and how infinitely
greater would be the enjoyment of a gifted boy like
Chopin when, unburdened by school exercises, he
can wander through wood and meadow, dreaming of
fairies and wood-nymphs. Frederic, who was not
at all fond of long, fatiguing walks, loved to lie
under a tree, and indulge in beautiful day-dreams.
Instead of an ordinary correspondence it occurred to
him to bring out a little periodical under the title of
the *Kurjer Szafarski*, on the model of the *Warsaw
Courier*, a paper then published in the capital.
Among the memorials of Frederic, collected by the
family are two numbers of this little journal, for
the year 1824. At the beginning of the first number
we read: "On July 15th, M. Pichon (a name
Frederic assumed) appeared at the musical assembly
at Szafarnia, at which were present several persons,
big and little : he played Kalkbrenner's Concerto,
but this did not produce such a *furore*, especially

among the youthful hearers, as the song which the same gentleman rendered." It happened that a great many Jews were at that time in the neighbouring village of Oborów (the property of M. Romocki) to buy grain. Frederic invited some of them to his room, and played to them a kind of Jewish wedding March, called "Majufes." His performance excited such enthusiasm among his guests that they not only began to dance, but earnestly begged him to come to an approaching Jewish marriage, and give them some more of his exquisite music. " He plays," said the delighted Israelites, " like a born Jew." *

The remainder of the news of the *Kurjer Szfarski* consisted of humorous descriptions of the daily events of the village. A strange glimpse of the condition of Poland is afforded by the fact, that according to a custom, which even now prevails in Warsaw, each issue of this journal was examined by the government censor, whose business it was to write on every number, "lawful for transmission." The office was at that time held by Mlle. Louise Dziewanowska, daughter of the proprietor of Szafarnia.

It would be impossible to enumerate all the jokes and harmless mysteries which this famous man indulged in during the happy days of boyhood, but

---

* This story is given by Wladislaus Casimir Wocicki in his work entitled " Cmentarz Powazkowski."

I will mention a few of his merry tricks, for the sake of those who linger with affectionate interest over his early years.

Mons. Romocki, the proprietor of Oborów, once sold his wheat to a Jewish merchant. Hearing of the purchase, Frederic wrote a letter in the Polo-Jewish style, purporting to come from the buyer, and stating that, after mature consideration, he found he should be a loser by the bargain, and, therefore, declined it. The writing was abominable, the spelling full of blunders, but the deception succeeded so well that Romocki was in a frightful rage. He sent for the Jew instantly, and would probably have soundly belaboured the unfortunate merchant had not Frederic confessed his mischievous trick in time. Romocki laughed at the joke, and was on his guard against being taken in again by Frederic. The deeper meaning underlying all the acts of this accomplished man in later years showed itself even here. Romocki was ashamed of his fury, and it is said from that day he very rarely, and only from necessity, took a whip in his hand.

Between 1820 and 1830 there was an Evangelical pastor in Warsaw, named Tetzner, who preached every Sunday in German and Polish alternately, and from his defective knowledge of the language, proclaimed the truths of the gospel in very broken Polish. Being led into his church from curiosity, Frederic was at once struck by the droll speech of the preacher, and carefully noticed every wrongly

pronounced word.   When he reached home, he
constructed a kind of pulpit with tables and chairs,
put on a whig, and, summoning the family, delivered
'a discourse in imitation of the pastor's broken
Polish, which was so ludicrous that his hearers
burst into roars of laughter.

If his father's pupils made too much noise in the
house, Frederic had only to place himself at the
piano to produce instant and perfect quiet.   One day
when Professor Chopin was out there was a frightful scene.   Barcinski, the master present, was at
his wits' end, when Frederic, happily, entered the
room.*   Without deliberation he requested the rois-
terers to sit down, called in those who were making
a noise outside, and promised to improvise an interesting story on the piano, if they would be quite
quiet.   All were instantly as still as death, and
Frederic sat down to the instrument and extin-
guished the lights.†   He described how robbers
approached a house, mounted by ladders to the
windows, but were frightened away by a noise
within.   Without delay they fled on the wings of
the wind into a deep, dark wood, where they fell

---

* One of these pupils, Casimir Wodzynski, a property
owner, who is still living, often tells this story.

† Chopin generally improvised in the dark, frequently at
night, as then the mind is undisturbed by outward impressions.
Then he would bury himself in the theme heart and soul, and
develope from it tone-pictures full of lofty inspiration and fairy-
like poetry.

asleep under the starry sky. He played more and more softly, as if trying to lull children to rest, till he found that his hearers had actually fallen asleep. The young artist noiselessly crept out of the room, to his parents and sisters, and asked them to follow him with a light. When the family had amused themselves with the various postures of the sleepers, Frederic sat down again to the piano, and struck a thrilling chord, at which they all sprang up in a fright. A hearty laugh was the *finale* of this musical joke.

Further on in his life we meet with a companion picture to this story, which affords us an excellent example of Frederic's talent for improvisation, profound knowledge of counterpoint, and mastery over all technical difficulties. Like all gifted and accomplished musicians, he showed an especial preference for the organ as offering wide scope for the freest improvisation. It was customary for the students of the Warsaw University to assemble about eleven in the morning for service at the Wizytek Church, at which artists and *dilettanti* performed vocal masses with and without orchestral accompaniments.

Chopin somtimes sat in the choir and played the organ. One day when the celebrant had sung the " Oremus," Frederic improvised, in a highly ingenious manner, on the motive of the portion of the mass already performed, working out the fundamental thought with the most interesting combinations and contrapuntal devices. The choristers and band, spell-bound by the magic power of his fancy, left their desks, and surrounded the player, listening with rapt attention, as if they had been in the concert room rather than the church. The priest, at the altar, patiently awaited the conclusion, but the sacristan rushed angrily into the choir, exclaiming: "what the d—— are you doing? The priest has twice intoned, *Per omnia sæcula sæculorum*, the ministrant has rung repeatedly, and still you keep on playing. The superior who sent me is out of all patience." Chopin awoke from his reverie, and his hands lay motionless on the keys. Although his wonderful improvisations generally cost him but little trouble, he spared no pains when preparing a work for publication. When absorbed by a thought he would brood over it for hours and days in perfect silence and solitude. What passed in the soul of the tone-poet at these seasons cannot be described; with such psychological conditions the imaginative can sympathise, and all who are sensible to the influences of poetry and art may in some measure understand.

Chopin had an instrument in his bed-room, and often worked far on into the night; sometimes when the rest of the household were asleep, he would spring out of bed, rush to his piano, and strike a few chords, developing some immatured thought, or resolving some imperfect harmony. Then he would lie down, but only to rise and do the same thing again, daylight frequently finding him thus occupied.

The servants, by whom Frederic was much beloved, but who could not understand such proceedings, shook their heads compassionately, and said, "The poor young gentleman's mind is affected."

When on an excursion with his father to the suburbs, or spending his holidays in the country, he always listened attentively to the song of the reaper, and the tune of the peasant fiddler, fixing in his memory and delighting to idealise these frequently original and expressive melodies. He often wondered who was the creator of the beautiful melodies inter-woven in the Mazurkas, Cracoviennes, and Polo-naises, and how the Polish peasants learnt to sing and play the violin with such purity. No one could give him any information. Indeed both the words and melodies of these songs are the creation of several minds. An artless, spontaneous melody, poured forth by one person, is altered, and perhaps improved, by another, and so passes from mouth to mouth till finally it becomes a possession of all the people. Slavonic folk-songs differ greatly from the Romance and Germanic ; they are historical records of the feelings, customs, and character of the people.*

Chopin was born and bred in Mazovia, a peculi-

---

* Another kind of national song is the product of the trained musician, and being, from its original, majestic, war-like or sentimental character, easily understandable, it is readily remembered and rapidly diffused. Everyone sings it to the

arly music-loving province. A distinguished Polish writer † says : " The love of song characterizes the Slavonic above all other races ; the rudest peasant could be allured to the end of the world by his national songs." The Mazovians have such an intense love for music that they sing about the commonest affairs of life, readily perceiving their pleasing and touching phases. The predilection of the Poles for these songs is often a matter of pecuniary profit, for a beggar, with some talent in singing and playing the violin, has no difficulty in obtaining alms. During the great festivals—Easter, Whitsuntide, and Christmas — men and women walk about the Mazovian villages, singing and playing appropriate dances, and everywhere they are warmly received, gladly listened to, and not sparingly rewarded. Nearly all these songs originated in the cottage, their composers were men who could neither read nor write, and whose names will always remain unknown.

Poetical perception and sensibility to the beauties of nature are evidently innate in the Polish character; they are susceptibilities which neither prosaic

---

best of his ability; but the less-educated, even when they delight in a work of art, seldom inquire who created it. For example, many people are not aware that Henry Carey was the author and composer of " God Save the King."

† Julian Klaczko, a contributor to the *Revue des Deux Mondes.*

work, the cares of daily life, nor even the burden of more than a century of national suffering have had power to blunt.

In his childhood Chopin had imbedded these folk-songs in his memory, and, impressed by their peculiar beauty, he frequently interwove some especial favorite into his own compositions. He first gave the national dance tune a truly beautiful and perfect form by adorning it with interesting harmonies and poetical arabesques.

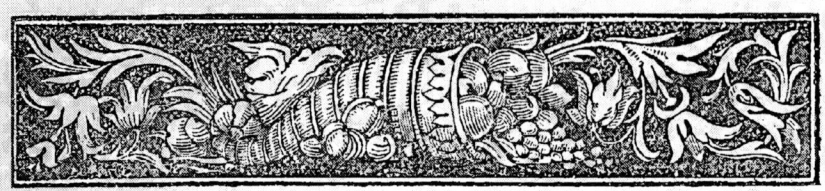

CHAPTER III.

CHOPIN'S EARLY MANHOOD. HIS FIRST JOURNEY.
HIS RELATIONS WITH PRINCE ANTON
RADZIWILL.

THE year 1825 found Frederic's social and artistic circle continually increasing in numbers and influence, and the fame of his extraordinary musical talents spreading far and wide. He excited universal interest, and it is a proof of his popularity that the only strikingly successful concerts were those in which he took part. His marvellous playing at two grand concerts, given for charitable objects, in the hall of the Conservatoire, on May 27th, and June 10th, 1825, awakened unbounded approbation. As the best pianist in the capital, Chopin was summoned to play before the Emperor, Alexander I., who, during his stay in Warsaw, was desirous of hearing the newly-invented Aelomelodicon.* The instrument was placed in the Protestant Church, for the sake of heightening the tone by its being heard

---

* Brunner and Hoffman were the inventors.

under the enormous dome of that building. In
token of his admiration of the wonderful performance of the talented youth, then little more than a
boy, the Emperor presented him with a valuable
diamond ring.

The same year saw the publication of Chopin's
first printed work, the Rondo dedicated to Madame
von Linde.   Neither this nor the following " Rondo
à la Masur," op. 5, also published in Warsaw, made
him famous abroad, but in his own city he was
already regarded as a popular and rapidly ripening
artist.   Looking at their son merely as a dis-
tinguised *dilettante*, his parents had not made music
his chief study, but when they saw that Frederic
was by nature designed for a great musician, they
removed all obstacles, and left him to the undisturbed enjoyment of his piano and his poetic dreams.

Everywhere he was warmly welcomed : in the
drawing-rooms of the aristocracy, by his comrades at
the Conservatoire, or the Lyceum, of which he was
considered the highest ornament, and where he formed
some life-long friendships.   Among these friends we
may mention Titus Woyciechowski, to whom he
dedicated his " Variations, op. 2 ; " Alexander Rembielinski ; * Wilhelm von Kolberg ; Johann Matuszynski, Stanislas Kozmian, now President of the
Scientific Society at Posen ; Eustachius Marylski ;

---

* Alexander Rembielinski, an excellent pianist, who died
young.

Dominicus Magnuszewski and Stephan Witwicki, both poets of talent; Celinski; Hube, and Julius Fontana.*

Frederic excited no jealousy among his fellow students at the Conservatoire, for his talents as pianist and composer were so pre-eminent that they all bowed before him as their master. Kind and affable by disposition he had also an innate grace, while, from his education and refined surroundings, he possessed, even in early youth, the tact of a grown-up person. These qualities won the esteem and affection of all who knew him, and no one was offended by his practical jokes, mimicries, or caricatures.

The activity of the young artist was intense, and although his excessive exertions appeared to him but slight, they undoubtedly injured his delicate

---

* Julius Fontana, pianist and composer, was born in Warsaw, in 1810, and educated with Chopin at the Conservatoire, under Elsner. In 1830 he entered the army and soon became a lieutenant of artillery. After the insurrection he emigrated to France; some years later settled in America, but in 1850 returned to Paris, where he died in 1870. He was an almost daily guest of Chopin's, and knew exactly what compositions were published at that time; the facts that he gives in the preface to his edition of Chopin's works are, therefore, trustworthy. Besides many smaller compositions, (Walzes Studies. Caprices, Fantasias) which he wrote and published in Paris, he published "Polish National Melodies" (London); "Comments on Polish Orthography" (Leipsic, 1866); and "Popular Astronomy" (Posen, 1869.)

constitution. Frederic's parents having been advised by the physicians to send their youngest daughter, Emily, to Bad Reinerz, in Silesia, they thought it well to let him accompany her that he might try the whey cure. Accordingly, at the beginning of the holidays of 1826, the mother, Louise, Emily, and Frederic went to the then much frequented spring. During their visit a poor widow, who had vainly been seeking help from the healing stream, died, leaving two young children, under the care of a faithful nurse, but without sufficient means for the funeral and the journey home. Hearing of their need, Chopin made the noblest use of his talents. He arranged a concert for the benefit of the poor children, and had the satisfaction of obtaining a good sum. By his masterly playing he won the admiration of the connoisseurs ; by his benevolence, the esteem of all generous minds. He became the object of the most courteous attention. A few days after the concert Frederic and his family left Reinerz, and spent the rest of the summer at the village of Strzyzewo, part of the estate of his god-mother, Madame von Wiesiolowska, sister to Count Skarbek.

Prince Anton Radziwill, a wealthy nobleman, related to the Prussian Royal family, and Governor of the Duchy of Posen, had his summer residence in the neighbouring village, Antonin. A passionate lover of music, a keen connoisseur, and a thoroughly trained composer, he had obtained celebrity by his music to the first part of Goethe's *Faust*, which, by Royal command, was for several years performed annually in his honour at the Berlin Academy for Singing.   He had a very agreeable tenor voice, and also played the violoncello well.   His house, in Posen, was the *rendezvous* for the best artists, and quartet parties for the performance of classical music were held in his *salons* nearly every week, the Prince himself playing the violoncello.

Frederic having availed himself of an invitation to Antonin, the Prince took a great fancy to him, and was charmed with his playing.   In May, 1829, when he went to Warsaw as representative of the Prussian court, at the coronation of the Emperor Nicholas, he visited Frederic at his father's house, and was very pressing in inviting him to his establishment at Posen.   There was no further personal intercourse between this magnate and our artist, yet writers, ignorant of the facts, have represented the Prince as Chopin's benefactor, and as having supplied the means for his education.   Franz Liszt was the first to promulgate this error in his book, entitled " Francois Chopin," written in French, shortly after the master's death, in which he says, " supplementing the limited means of the family, the Prince bestowed on Frederic the inestimable gift of a good and complete education.   Through a friend, M. Antoine Korzuchowski, the Prince, whose own elevated mind enabled him to understand the requirements of an artistic career, always paid his

educational expenses.   From this time until the
death of Chopin, M. Korzuchowski held the closest
relations of friendship with him." In this statement
there is not a word of truth, yet it has been repeated
not only by foreign, but, what is less pardonable, even
by Polish authors.

We are fully aware that in the portions of the
work relating to Chopin's youth, manners, compositions, and to the Polish national music, Liszt
received much help from a Polish emigrant, Franz
Grzymala.   He had been a deputy at the Diet,
and was an able author and journalist ; he died
in Paris in 1871, the day after the capitulation.
Not having made Chopin's acquaintance until his
residence in Paris, it does not appear, from what
he told Liszt, that he could have possessed any
accurate information about his early life.   Julius
Fontana, who had known Chopin from childhood,
entered a protest against Liszt's assertion, so also
did the parents of the great artist, who were sadly
pained to read that Prince Radziwill had entirely
provided for Frederic's education.   Professor at
three large academies in Warsaw, and proprietor
of a flourishing *pension*, surely Nicholas Chopin
would have found means for the education of his
dearly loved and only son.

An equally untrue report has been spread to the
effect that Chopin travelled to Italy at the expense
of Prince Radziwill.   In reality the expenses of
the journey were defrayed by the receipts of three

numerously attended concerts given in Warsaw.
The first time he asked his father for money was
when he had determined on going to Paris, after a
sojourn of eighteen months in the beautiful Austrian
capital.   In his charming, child-like manner, he
lamented that he should be the cause of additional
expenditure to his parents, to whom he had, he
thought, already cost quite enough.   His father
sent him the money, and an affectionate letter, ex-
pressing his willingness to supply him with means,
until he procured some regular mode of subsistence
in Paris.

As a mark of friendship and respect for the distinguished composer of the music to *Faust*, Frederic
dedicated to him his Trio, for pianoforte and violoncello, op. 8, composed in Warsaw between 1827 and
1829; so that in point of fact Chopin, not the
Prince, was the donor.   It is only fair to Liszt to
say that he is less to blame for the circulation of
the error we have pointed out, than Grzymala and
those who blindly believed and promulgated a statement so utterly false.

CHAPTER IV.

THE JOURNEY TO BERLIN. CHOPIN'S LETTERS.
AN INCIDENT OF THE RETURN TO WARSAW.

IN 1827 Chopin passed his final examination before leaving the Lyceum, not, however, with such brilliant success as on former occasions, when every promotion to a higher class had been accompanied by a special reward. This is accounted for by his having, during the last year, devoted his chief energies to music, a goodly pile of compositions, finished or sketched in outline, being found in his study. Elsner, who was the keenest observer and most competent judge of Frederic's artistic progress, and creative power, exhorted his parents to let their son have his own way, and to do all they could to encourage his lofty flights of fancy.

The question now was how to give the young composer better opportunities for hearing and studying than his native city afforded. Although first-rate artists occasionally gave concerts in Warsaw, Frederic could only satisfy his ardent desire of hearing the sublime works of the classic masters,

in the larger European centres of life and intelligence. His parents, therefore, resolved to send
their beloved son to Vienna or Berlin, if only for
a few weeks, at the very first favourable opportunity.
One soon offered. In 1828, Professor Jarocki, having
been invited by Alexander von Humboldt to the
Naturalists' Congress, at Berlin, Nicholas Chopin
was only too happy to confide his son to the care
of one of his best friends, while the Professor was
equally pleased to have the company of an amiable
and talented young man like Chopin.

Thus he left his native land for the first time
to visit a large foreign city, where he hoped to learn
a great deal. Unconscious of his own artistic greatness he had no wish to appear in Berlin as a pianist
or composer. An opportunity was offered him of
meeting Spontini, Zelter, and the youthful though
famous Felix Mendelssohn, but he did not venture
to present himself before these celebrated masters.
The physiognomies of the German *savants* seemed
odd to the young Pole, the French blood stirred in
his veins, and he could not refrain from caricaturing
these worthy but somewhat strange-looking gentlemen.

He was enraptured with the oratorio of Handel's,
which he heard at the Academy of Singing : never
had he received so deep an impression from church
music. The performance of *Der Freischutz*, with
which bewitching opera he had already become acquainted in Warsaw, likewise gave him indescribable

delight, while he was much interested in comparing the opera in that city with the Royal opera in Berlin.

Since he left Warsaw the only time he touched the piano was at a little village on his way back, when he played at the request of the post master and his travelling companions.

We will now let our artist speak for himself, only making such alterations as the necessities of translation require.

To Titus Woyciechowsky.
Warsaw, September 9th, 1828.

DEAREST TITUS,

You cannot think how I have been longing for news of you and your mother, nor imagine my joy when I received your letter. I was then at Strzyzewo, where I spent the whole summer, but could not reply immediately because I was so busy preparing to return to Warsaw. Now I am writing like a lunatic, for I really do not know what I am about. I am actually starting for Berlin to-day! There is to be a philosophical congress at Berlin—after the model of those held in Switzerland and Bavaria — to which the King has requested the University to invite the most celebrated European naturalists. The president is to be the renowned Alexander von Humboldt. Professor Jarocki has received an invitation as a zoologist, and ex-student and doctor of the Berlin University. Something magnificent is anticipated. and it is reported that Spontini will give a performance of his " Cortez."

Jarocki's friend and teacher, Lichtenstein, officiates as secretary to the Congress : he is a member of the Academy of Singing, and is on a friendly footing with the director, Herr Zelter. I learn from a good authority in Berlin that I shall have an opportunity, through Lichtenstein, of becoming acquainted with all the best musicians in the Prussian capital, except Spontini, with whom he is not on good terms.

I shall be much pleased to meet the Prussian Prince Radziwill, who is a friend of Spontini. I only intend spending a fortnight with Jarocki, but this will give me an opportunity of, at any rate, hearing a good opera once, and so having an idea of a perfect performance, which is worth a good deal of trouble.

At Strzyzewo I arranged my last Rondo in C major, for two pianos.*

To-day I tried it with Ernemann, at Bucholtz's,† and it came out pretty well. We intend to play it some day at the " Ressource."

As to new compositions I have nothing besides the still unfinished Trio (G minor) which I began after your departure. The first *Allegro* I have already tried with accompaniments.

---

* It appears as op. 73, in Fontana's collection of the posthumous works.

† Ernemann was a music master, and Bucholtz a pianoforte maker, in Warsaw.

It seems to me that this Trio will meet the same fate as the Sonata and Variations. Both are already in Vienna; the former I have dedicated to Elsner, as his pupil; to the latter I have—perhaps somewhat presumptuously—affixed your name. I acted on the impulse of affection, and I am sure you will not misconstrue my motives. Skarbek has not yet returned, Jedrzejewicz will remain some time longer in Paris.* He was there introduced to the pianist Sowinski,† who wrote to me to say that he should like to make my acquaintance, by correspondence, before he comes to Warsaw. As he is assistant editor of Fétis's *Revue Musicale*, he would be glad to be informed about musical affairs in Poland, or to receive biographies of the foremost Polish composers and artists—matters in which I have not the least intention of being mixed up, so I shall reply to him from Berlin that what he wants is not at all in my line, and that I do not feel competent to write for a Paris journal, requiring able and matured criticism.

At the end of this month I shall leave Berlin, a five days' journey by diligence!

Everything here is just the same as ever; the excellent *Zywny* is the heart and soul of all our parties.

---

* Professor Jedrzejewicz, Chopin's brother-in-law, born 1803, died in Warsaw, 1853.

† A composer, pianist, and *littérateur*, who is still living in P

I must conclude, for my luggage is already packed and sent to the diligence.

I kiss your mother's feet and hands. My parents and sisters send kind regards and sincerest wishes for the improvement of her health.

Take pity on me, and write soon, however briefly. I shall value a single line.

Yours,
FREDERIC.

———

Berlin, Tuesday.*

MY DEARLY BELOVED PARENTS
            AND SISTERS,

We arrived safely in this great city about 3 o'clock on Sunday afternoon, and went direct from the post to the hotel " Zum Kronprinz," where we are now. It is a good and comfortable house. The day we arrived Professor Jarocki took me to Herr Lichtenstein's, where I met Alex. von Humboldt. He is not above the middle height, and his features cannot be called handsome, but the prominent, broad brow, and the deep penetrating glance reveal the searching intellect of the scholar, who is as great a philanthropist as he is a traveller. He speaks French like his mother tongue; even you would have said so, dear Father.

---

* September 16th, 1828.

Herr Lichtenstein promised to introduce me to the first musicians here; and regretted that we had not arrived a few days sooner to have heard his daughter perform at a *matinée*, last Sunday, with orchestral accompaniments.

I, for my part, felt but little disappointment, but, whether rightly or wrongly, I know not, for I have neither seen nor heard the young lady. The day we arrived there was a performance of "The Interrupted Sacrifice,"* but our visit to Herr Lichtenstein prevented me from being present.

Yesterday the savants had a grand dinner; Herr von Humboldt did not occupy the chair, but a very different looking person, whose name I cannot at this moment recall. However, as he is, no doubt, some celebrity, I have written his name under my portrait of him. (I could not refrain from making some caricatures, which I have already classified.) The dinner lasted so long that there was not time for me to hear Birnbach, the much-praised violinist of nine years. To-day I shall dine alone, having made my excuses to Professor Jarocki, who readily perceived that, to a musician, the performance of such a work as Spontini's "Ferdinand Cortez," must be more interesting than an interminable

---

* Peter von Winter, born at Mannheim, in 1755, died at Munich, 1825, was a popular and rather over-rated composer. This opera made a great sensation.

dinner among philosophers. Now I am quite alone, and enjoying a chat with you, my dear ones.

There is a rumour that the great Paginini is coming here. I only hope it is true. Prince Radziwill is expected on the 20th of this month. It will be a great pleasure to me if he comes. I have, as yet, seen nothing but the *Zoological Cabinet*, but I know the city pretty well, for I wandered among the beautiful streets and bridges for two whole days. You shall have a verbal description of these, as, also, of the large and decidedly beautiful castle. The chief impression Berlin makes upon me is that of a straggling city which could, I think, contain double its present large population. We wanted to have stayed in the French street, but I am very glad we did not, for it is as broad as our Lezno,* and needs ten times as many people as are in it to take off its desolate appearance.

To-day will be my first experience of the music of Berlin. Do not think me one-sided, dearest Papa, for saying that I would much rather have spent the morning at Schlesinger's than in labouring through the thirteen rooms of the Zoological Museum, but I came here for the sake of my musical education, and Schlesinger's library, containing, as it does, the most important musical works of every age and

---

* A long wide street in Warsaw.

country, is, of course, of more interest to me than
any other collection. I console myself with the
thought that I shall not miss Schlesinger's, and that
a young man ought to see all he can, as there is
something to be learnt everywhere. This morning
I went to Kisting's pianoforte manufactory, at the
end of the long Frederic Street, but as there was
not a single instrument completed, I had my long
walk in vain. Fortunately for me there is a good
grand piano in our hotel, which I play on every day,
both to my own and the landlord's gratification.

The Prussian diligences are most uncomfortable,
so the journey was less agreeable than I had
anticipated; however, I reached the capital of the
Hohenzollerns in good health and spirits. Our
travelling companions were a German lawyer, living
at Posen, who tried to distinguish himself by making
coarse jokes; and a very fat farmer, with a smatter-
ing of politeness acquired by travelling.

At the last stage before Frankfort-on-the-Oder,
a German Sappho entered the diligence and poured
forth a torrent of ridiculous, egotistical complaints.
Quite unwittingly, the good lady amused me immensely, for it was as good as a comedy, when she
began to argue with the lawyer, who, instead of
laughing at her, seriously controverted everything
she said.

The suburbs of Berlin, on the side by which we
approached are not pretty, but the scrupulous clean-
liness and order which everywhere prevail are very

pleasing to the eye. To-morrow I shall visit the suburbs on the other side.

The Congress will commence its sittings the day after to-morrow, and Herr Lichtenstein has promised me a ticket. In the evening Alex. von Humboldt will receive the members at his house : Professor Jarocki offered to procure me an invitation, but I thanked him and said I should gain little, if any, intellectual advantage from such a gathering, for which I was not learned enough ; besides the professional gentlemen might cast questioning glances at a layman like me, and ask, " Is Saul then among the prophets ? " I fancied, even at the dinner, that my neighbour, Professor Lehmann, a celebrated botanist from Hamburg, looked at me rather curiously.. I was astonished at the strength of his small fist ; he broke with ease the large piece of white bread, to divide which I was fain to use both hands and a knife. He leaned over the table to talk to Professor Jarocki, and in the excitement of the conversation mistook his own plate and began to drum upon mine. A real *savant*, was he not ? with the great ungainly nose, too. All this time I was on thorns, and as soon as he had finished with my plate, I wiped off the marks of his fingers with my serviette as fast as possible.

Marylski cannot have an atom of taste if he thinks the Berlin ladies dress well ; their clothes are handsome, no doubt, but alas for the beautiful stuffs cut up for such puppets ! Your ever fondly loving,

FREDERIC.

D

Berlin, September 20th, 1828.

I am well and happy, dear Parents and Sisters.
As if on purpose to honour me, a fresh piece is
brought out at the theatre every day. First I heard
an oratorio at the Academy of Singing; then at
the Opera, "Ferdinand Cortez," "Il Matrimonio
Segreto," and Onslow's * " Der Hausirer." I greatly
enjoyed all these performances, but I must confess
that I was quite carried away by Handel's "Ode on
St. Cecilia's Day;" this most nearly approaches
my ideal of sublime music. With the exception of
Signora Tibaldi (alto), and Fräulein von Schätzel,
whom I heard in "Der Hausirer," and at the
Academy of Singing, all the best singers are away.
Fräulein von Schätzel pleased me best in the
Oratorio, but it may have been that I was in
a better mood that evening for listening. The
Oratorio, however, was not without a " but," which,
perhaps, will only be got rid of in Paris.

I have not called on Herr Lichtenstein yet, for he
is so busy with preparations for the Congress, that
even Professor Jarocki can scarcely get a word with
him, but he has kindly procured me a ticket of
admission. I was in such a capital place that I

---

* George Onslow, born in 1744, at Clermont-Ferrand, was
descended from a noble English family. He was a pupil of
Cramer and Dussek, and besides operas, of which " Der
Hausirer" was the favourite, he wrote a great deal of chamber
music, especially some excellent quartets.

could see and hear everything, and was quite close to the Crown Prince. Spontini, Zelter, and Felix Mendelssohn Bartholdy were also there; but I did not speak to any of them, as I did not think it proper to introduce myself. It is said that Prince Radziwill will come to-day; I shall find out after breakfast if this is really true.

At the Singing Academy I observed the handsome Princess von Liegnitz, talking to a man in a kind of livery, whose face I could not clearly see. I asked my neighbour if he were a Royal valet de chambre, and received for a reply, " Aye, that is His Excellency Baron von Humboldt." You may imagine, my dear ones, how thankful I was that I had only uttered my question in a whisper; but I assure you that the chamberlain's uniform changes even the countenance, or I could not have failed to recognise the great traveller, who has ascended the mighty Chimborazo. Yesterday he was present at the performance of " Der Hausirer," or, as the French call it, " Le Colporteur." In the Royal box sat Prince Charles.

The day before yesterday we visited the Royal library, which is very large, but does not contain many musical works. I was much interested in seeing an autograph letter of Kosciusko's, which his biographer, Falkenstein, immediately copied, letter by letter. When he saw that we were Poles, and could, therefore, read the letter without any trouble, he begged Professor Jarocki to translate it into German, while he wrote it down in his pocket book.

Falkenstein, an agreeable young man, is secretary to the Dresden Library. I met, also, the editor of the *Berlin Musical Gazette;* we were introduced, and exchanged a few words. To-morrow will see the fulfilment of one of my most earnest wishes: " Der Freischutz" is to be performed. I shall then be able to compare our singers with the singers here. To-day I am invited to the grand dinner at the drill house. The number of caricatures increases.

Yours ever lovingly,

FREDERIC.

Berlin, Saturday, September 27th, 1828.

I am quite well, and have seen all that is to be seen. I shall soon be with you again. In a week, from the day after to-morrow, we shall embrace. Lounging about agrees with me capitally. Yesterday " The Interrupted Sacrifice " was performed again, and Fräulein von Schätzel omitted more than one chromatic scale. I quite fancied myself in your midst.* This "your" reminds me of a Berlin caricature.† A Napoleon grenadier stands as a sentinel; he calls out, " qui vive," to a woman

----

* A reference to the Warsaw lady singers, who often left out or altered *coloratures.*

† In Polish "your" is "wasz," pronounced "wasch" or " vache."

passing. She is about to reply, "die Wascherin" (the laundress), but wishing to express herself in a more refined manner, she says, "la vache" (the cow.) I count among the great events of my visit here the second dinner with the naturalists, which took place the day before the conclusion of the Congress, and was really very lively and entertaining. Several very fair convivial songs were sung, in which all the company joined more or less heartily. Zelter conducted, and a large golden cup, standing on a red pedestal, in front of him, as a sign of his exalted musical merits, appeared to give him much satisfaction. The dishes were better that day than usual, they say, "because the naturalists have been principally occupied during their sittings with the improvement of meats, sauces, soups, &c." They make fun of these learned gentlemen in like manner at the Konigstadt Theatre. In a play, in which some beer is drunk, one asks, "Why is beer so good now in Berlin?" "Why, because the naturalists are holding their conference," is the answer.

But it is time to go to bed, as we start off quite early to-morrow. We shall spend two days at Posen, on account of an invitation from the Archbishop Wolicki. Oh, how much I shall have to tell you, my dearests, and how glad I shall be to see you again.

Your warmly affectionate

FREDERIC.

Professor Jarocki and Chopin had, as companions, on their return from Berlin, two gentlemen, whose wearisome talk about politics, in which Chopin never took any interest, and still more their incessant smoking, (almost unendurable to Chopin) made them very disagreeable. When one of the gentlemen announced that he should smoke till he went to sleep, and would rather die than give up his pipe, Frederic and the Professor went outside the diligence to enjoy the fresh air.

At the little town of Züllichau, finding they had an hour to wait for horses, Professor Jarocki proposed a walk through the place. This did not take long, and as the horses were not ready when they returned, the Professor sat down to a meal—the post-house being also a restaurant—but Frederic, as if drawn by a magnet, went into the next room, and saw—oh, wonder of wonders!—a grand piano. Professor Jarocki, who could see through the open door, laughed to himself when his young friend opened the instrument, which had a very unpromising exterior; Chopin also looked at it with some misgivings; but when he had struck a few chords he exclaimed, in joyful surprise, " O Santa Cæcilia, the piano is in tune."

Only the impassioned musician knows what it is, after sitting for several days in a diligence, suddenly, and quite unexpectedly, to have an opportunity of playing on a good instrument.

Regardless of his surroundings our artist began to

improvise *con amore*.   Attracted by the music, one of
the travellers got up and stood behind the player's
chair.   Chopin called out to Professor Jarocki, in
Polish, " Now we shall see whether my listener be a
connoisseur or not." Frederic began his Fantasia on
Polish Songs (op. 13) ; the traveller, a German,
stood like one petrified, captivated by this music, so
new and bewitching ; his eyes mechanically followed
every movement of the pianist's delicate hand ; he
had forgotten everything, even his beloved pipe,
which went out unheeded.   The other travellers
stepped in softly, and at the same time the tall postmaster and his buxom wife appeared at the side
door with their two pretty daughters behind them.
Frederic, unmindful of his audience, and absorbed in
converse with his muse, had lost all thought of where
he was, and that he must soon be on his way.

More and more tender and graceful became his
playing ; the fairies seemed to be singing their moon-
light melodies ; everyone was listening in rapt
attention to the elegant arabesques sparkling from
his fingers, when a stentorian voice, which made the
windows rattle, called out, " The horses are ready,
gentlemen."

" Confounded disturber," roared the postmaster,
while the triplet of ladies cast angry glances at the
postilion.   Chopin sprang from his seat, but was
immediately surrounded by his audience, who exclaimed with one voice : " Go on, dear sir, finish
that glorious piece, which we should have heard all

through but for that tiresome man." " But," replied Chopin, consulting his watch, " we have already been here some hours, and are due in Posen shortly."

" Stay and play, noble young artist," cried the postmaster, " I will give you couriers' horses if you will only remain a little longer."

" Do be persuaded," began the postmaster's wife, almost threatening him with an embrace. What could Frederic do but sit down again to the instrument ?

When he paused the servant appeared with wine and glasses ; the daughters of the host served the artist first, then the other travellers, while the postmaster gave a cheer for the " darling Polyhymnias," as he expressed it, in which all united. One of the company (probably the town cantor) went close up to Chopin and said, in a voice trembling with emotion, " Sir, I am an old and thoroughly trained musician ; I, too, play the piano, and so know how to appreciate your masterly performance ; if Mozart had heard it he would have grasped your hand and cried, ' Bravo.' An insignificant old man like myself cannot dare to do so."

The women, in their gratitude, filled the pockets of the carriage with the best eatables that the house contained, not forgetting some good wine. The postmaster exclaimed, with tears of joy, " As long as I live I shall think, with enthusiasm, of Frederic Chopin."

When, after playing one more Mazurka, Frederic

prepared to go, his gigantic host seized him in his arms, and carried him to the carriage.

The postilion, still sulky over his scolding, and jealous because the pretty servant girl could not take her eyes off the interesting *virtuoso*, whispered to her, "Things often go very unfairly in the world. The young gentleman is carried into the carriage by the master himself; the like of us must climb laboriously on to the box by ourselves, though we are musical."

Long years afterwards Chopin would recall this episode with pleasure. It was like a good omen to him at the commencement of his artistic career. He often related how, like the old minstrels who went from town to town with their harps and received good cheer as their honorarium, he had played at Züllichau for cakes, fruit, and good wine; and assured his most intimate friends that the highest praise lavished on him by the press had never given him more pleasure than the naïve homage of the German who, in his eagerness to hear, let his pipe go out.

At Posen our travellers visited, by invitation, the Archbishop Wolicki, and paid their respects to Prince A. Radziwill. They both met with the kindest reception from the Prince, who knew how to esteem such a learned man as Jarocki, but, being a musician to the backbone, he was better able to appreciate the eminent talents of Chopin; he regarded him as a kindred spirit, whose superiority he

gladly recognized.   Most of the day was devoted
to music; the sonatas of Mozart, Beethoven, and
Hummel were performed by Chopin and the band-
master, Klinghor.   But Frederic called forth most
admiration by his incomparable improvisation.

As soon as they had left Posen, Frederic's ardent
yearning to see his family impelled him to his
father's house, and his love of art summoned him
back to his studies.   The last miles seemed endless,
and, yielding to his pressing request, the Professor
decided to take post horses at Lowicz.

On October 6th Frederic reached at length his
much desired goal.   His eyes, sparkling with
pleasure, rested on the towers of Warsaw, the
nimble horses flew along the street, the coach
stopped at the door, there were loud cries of joy,
and the dear returning one was in the loving arms of
his parents and sisters.

CHAPTER V.

JOURNEY TO VIENNA, PRAGUE, TEPLITZ, DRESDEN. CHOPIN'S PERFORMANCE AT TWO CONCERTS IN VIENNA.

FREDERIC studied with indefatigable zeal from one year's end to another; neither father nor teacher had ever been obliged to incite him to diligence, for even as a mere boy he had always shown a great desire for knowledge. But when the time approached for him to pass his final musical examination before a small critical circle, he worked almost beyond his strength. His anxious father, therefore, resolved to send him on another journey, having made the happy discovery that his Frederic had learned a great deal in Berlin.*

---

* In the summer of 1827, Chopin stayed for several weeks at his godmother's house, from whence he took a trip to Dantzig, to see the old trading city which used to belong to Poland. He wished also to make the acquaintance of the Superintendent Linde, brother of the Principal of the Warsaw Lyceum, at whose residence Frederic had already met the sisters of these gentlemen.

This time (July, 1829) our artist was to go to Vienna with some young friends, and he was highly delighted at the prospect, although his father and all his friends urged him to appear publicly as a pianist in that musical city.

With the innate modesty which never left him even after his greatest triumphs, he exclaimed, "Here I have been leniently judged by kind-hearted compatriots; but what am I to expect in a city which can boast of having heard a Haydn, a Mozart, and a Beethoven?"

A few months before this journey Frederic had become acquainted with Hummel, who had stayed some time in Warsaw, and given concerts there. Hummel* had acquired, by his very successful tour, the reputation of being the greatest living pianist. Chopin was acquainted with his compositions, and thought very highly of them. He greatly admired his classical style of playing, formed on the best models; yet, exacting as the young artist was towards himself, he could say, without vanity, that, in technical execution, he was not very inferior to the older master.

Frederic's chief desire was to become acquainted with the beautiful, musical Vienna, to hear all he could that was new to him, and, if possible, to have intercourse with the masters of his art. He never

---

* J. N. Hummel, born in Pressburg, November 14th, 1782; died in Weimar, October 17th, 1837.

dreamt that the latter, dazzled by his extraordinary genius, would be the very people who would press him to appear in public.

With a heart full of hope for himself and fervent blessings for his family, Chopin, in company with his friends Celinski, Hube, and Franz Maciejowski (the last named a nephew of the famous investigator of Slavonic law), left his beloved Warsaw.

After visiting Cracow, the old capital of the Piasts and the Jagellons and Ojcow, the so-called Polish Switzerland, the travellers arrived on July 31st at Vienna.

The following is a faithful transcription of the letters Chopin wrote from that city :—

Vienna, August 1st, 1829.

MY DEARLY LOVED PARENTS
        AND SISTERS,

We arrived here yesterday well and in good spirits, and I may say without fatigue, and so without discomfort. We took a private carriage at Cracow, in which we were very comfortable. We were able to enjoy to perfection the picturesque scenery of Galicia, Upper Silesia, and Moravia, for the clouds' had been amiable enough to lay the dust with a slight shower.

But before I speak of Vienna I must tell you about our journey to Ojcow. On Sunday afternoon we hired a four-horse country waggon, such as they use at Cracow, which cost us four thalers. We

dashed merrily and swiftly along to Ojcow, intend-
ing to put up at Herr Indyk's house, which all
tourists praise, and where Fräulein Tanska* stayed.
But, as ill-luck would have it, Herr Indyk lived a
full mile outside the town ; our coachman did not
know the way, and drove us into a little brook, as
clear and silvery as those in the fairy tales. Right
and left were walls of rock, and we did not find our
way out of the labyrinth till nearly 9 o'clock, when
two passing peasants good naturedly conducted us
to Herr Indyk's. Wearied and wet through, we at
length reached the wished for house, and were very
kindly received. Although not expecting visitors at
so late an hour, Herr Indyk made no trouble about
giving us a room in the little house, built on purpose
for tourists. Sister Isabella† Fräulein Tanska had
been in it only a little while before.

My companions changed their clothes and gathered
round the stove, in which our host had, meanwhile,
lighted a fire. Wet above the knees, I crouched in
a corner, considering what I had best do. Seeing
the mistress go into the next room for linen for our
beds, I instinctively followed her, and finding on the
table a pile of woollen Cracow caps (they are double
woven), I bought one, tore it in half, wrapped my

---

* Clementine Tanska, a famous Polish authoress for the
young.

† Chopin's second sister; she and her husband, M. Barcinski,
are still living in Warsaw.

feet in it, sat before the fire and drank a small glass of red wine. I thus escaped a severe cold. We laughed and talked a little while over our adventure, then went to bed and slept soundly.

———

Frederic, who had a sharp eye and a keen ear for all around him, goes on to describe the neighbourhood of Ojcow, the strangely-formed sand rocks, the black grotto, and the King's grotto, in which tradition says, that King Lokietek* took refuge from his enemies, at the end of the 13th century. Frederic was very enthusiastic over everything he saw, but Cracow and the neighbourhood appear to have had a special charm for him. He gives an account, also, of the Vienna picture gallery, to which he had at first only paid a flying visit. We give, unabridged, the following letters to his family :—

Vienna, August 8th, 1829.

I am well and in good spirits. Why, I do not know, but the people here are astonished at me, and I wonder at them for finding anything to wonder at in me. I am indebted to good Elsner's letter of recommendation for my exceedingly friendly reception by Herr Haslinger. He did not know how to

———

* A nickname given to this prince on account of his extraordinary small stature, in spite of which he was one of the most able rulers. A thorough exploration of the King's Grotto has recently been made by archæologists, and the bones of prehistoric animals discovered.

make me sufficiently welcome; he showed me all the musical novelties he had, made his son play to me, and apologized for not introducing his wife, who had just gone out. In spite of all his politeness he has not yet printed my compositions. I did not ask him about them, but he said, when showing me one of his finest editions, that my Variations were to appear, next week, in the same style, in *Odeon*. This I certainly had not expected.* He strongly advised me to play in public, although it is summer, and, therefore, not a favourable time for concerts.

The artists and lovers of music, who know that I am here, consider that Vienna would lose a great deal if I left without giving a concert. I do not know what to make of it all; Schuppanzigh, to whom I have letters of recommendation, informs me that although his quartet parties are over, he will try to get a gathering before I leave. I have only been once to Herr Hussarzewski; he was quite enthusiastic about my playing, and invited me to, dinner. Several Viennese gentlemen were present, and all, without exception, as if by previous concert, recommended me to perform in public.

Stein offered to send me one of his instruments, and begged me to play on it at my concert; Graff, whose pianos I prefer, has made the same proposal.

---

* Chopin had sent Haslinger for publication, the Variations on " La ci darem la mano," op. 2 ; and the Sonata, op. 4.

Würfel * says that if you have composed anything
new, and want it to create a sensation, you must,
by all means, play it yourself. Herr Blahetka, a
journalist, whom I met at Haslinger's, also advised
me to give a concert. My Variations have been
much praised by those who have heard them.

I have also made the acquaintance of Count
Gallenberg, who is manager of a theatre, where
I have heard some second-rate concerts. Haslinger
thinks that the Viennese should hear me play my
own compositions. Everybody assures me that the
newspapers will be sure to give me a flattering
notice. Würfel is of opinion that, as my compositions
are to appear now, it would be advisable for me to
give a concert, otherwise I should have to come
again, but that the present would be the best time,
as the Viennese are longing for something new. He
calls it unpardonable in a young musician to neglect
such an opportunity; I ought to appear in the two-
fold capacity of pianist and composer, and must not
think too modestly of myself. He wishes me to play
the Variations first, then the Rondo Cracovienne,
and, in conclusion, to improvise.

I do not know yet how it will all be arranged.
Stein is very kind and amiable, but I should prefer

---

* Wilhelm Würfel, born in Bohemia, was, for some years,
pianoforte teacher at the Warsaw Conservatoire. In 1826, he
became conductor at the Kärthner Thor Theatre, in Vienna,
where he died in 1832.

to use one of Graff's instruments. Haslinger, Blahetka and Würfel approve my choice.

Wherever I show myself, I am besieged with requests to play. I have no lack of acquaintances in the musical world, and Haslinger is going to introduce me to Charles Czerny. Up till now I have heard three operas, "La Dame Blanche," "Cenerentola," and Meyerbeer's "Crociato." Orchestra and chorus were excellent. To-day "Joseph in Egypt" is to be performed. I have twice listened, with admiration, to Mayseder's solos at the Academy of Music.

Vienna is handsome, lively, and pleases me exceedingly. They are trying to persuade me to spend the winter here. Würfel has just come in to take me to Haslinger's.

P.S.—I have made up my mind. Blahetka thinks I shall make a *furore*, for, as he puts it, I am "an artist of the first rank and worthy to be placed beside Moscheles, Herz, and Kalkbrenner." Würfel is really very kind, and has introduced me to Count Gallenberg; the bandmaster, Seyfried, and others of his influential acquaintances, and those who are interested in music. He declares I shall not leave Vienna till I have given a concert. Count Gallenberg is very pleased with this, as I shall play at his theatre, and—as my principal object now is to win laurels—without payment. The journalists stare at me already; the members of the orchestra salute me quite obsequiously when I walk in, arm in arm, with the director of the Italian opera (which is now closed.)

Würfel has taken no end of trouble on my behalf, and will be present at the rehearsal. He was very kind to me at Warsaw, and I am particularly glad that he has such a pleasant recollection of Elsner. People here are surprised that Kessler, Erncmann, and Czapeck should live in Warsaw with me there too, but I tell them that I give no lessons and only play from love of art. I have decided on Graff's instrument, but I do not want to offend Stein, so I shall thank him with such an expression of obligation that he cannot but forgive me.

I hope for God's gracious help. Do not be anxious, my dearest ones.

Your fondly loving

FREDERIC.

Vienna, Wednesday, August 12th, 1829.

You know of my intention, my beloved ones, from my last letter. Yesterday (Tuesday) at 7 o'clock in the evening, I appeared before a Viennese public for the first time, at the Imperial Opera House. Here, an evening concert in the theatre is called a musical academy. As I played gratuitously, Count Gallenberg expedited the arrangements for my appearance.

The following was the programme :

> Overture, by Beethoven
> My Variations.
> Song, by Fräulein Veltheim.*
> My Cracovienne.
> A Ballet, in conclusion.

The orchestra accompanied so badly at the rehearsal that I was obliged to substitute a " Free Fantasia " for the Rondo.

Directly I appeared I was greeted with cries of " Bravo," and, after each variation, the audience shouted this welcome word so lustily that I could not hear the *tutti* of the orchestra. I had such a hearty recall, that I was obliged to come forward twice to bow my acknowledgments. I must confess that I was not quite satisfied myself with the free fantasia ; but the public must have been pleased, for I was overwhelmed with applause. One reason for this may have been that the Germans know how to appreciate free improvisation. I am now doubly obliged to Würfel, for without his support and encouragement I should never have accomplished the daring stroke which has succeeded so well. I shall be able to relate my experiences and impressions by word of mouth better than I can now.

---

* Charlotte Veltheim was one of the most celebrated bravura singers of her time (1821—1840), and a much valued member of the Dresden Hof Theatre. She was a thorough musician, and played the piano very well.

I was not hissed, so don't be uneasy about my
artistic reputation. The newspapers have been very
favourable to me ; if some of them should pick holes
in me I am prepared for it. My compositions have
received Count Gallenberg's undivided approbation.
The theatrical manager, Herr Demar, was very
kind and pleasant ; he did his best to encourage me
before I appeared, so I went to my piano without
much anxiety.

My friends were scattered about that they might
hear the observations of the critics, and the various
opinions of the public. Celinski can tell you that he
heard nothing unfavourable. Hube reports the most
severe criticism, and that, too, from a lady : "A pity
the youth has so little presence." If this is the only
sort of blame I am to receive I cannot complain.
My friends swear they heard nothing but praise, and
that, until the spontaneous outburst of applause, not
one of them had clapped or uttered a bravo. The
manager was so pleased with my Rondo that he
came up after the concert, shook hands with me, and
made some very flattering remarks.

I improvised from " La Dame Blanche," and, that
I might have a Polish theme, chose " Chmiel." * The
public, to whom this kind of national melody is
quite unknown, seemed electrified. My spies in the

---

* " Chmiel " is a song in the mazurka measure, sung by the
Poles at marriage ceremonies at the moment when the bride's
sisters place the cap on her head.

pit say the people began a regular dance on the benches.

Wertheim, although only arriving yesterday with his wife from Carlsbad, went to the theatre; he could not imagine how I came to play there. He was here just now to congratulate me on my good success. At Carlsbad he saw Hummel who remembered me very kindly. He writes to him to-day, and will inform him of my performance.

Haslinger is to print my works; I have kept the programme of the concert. It was most interesting to me to become personally acquainted with Gyrowetz, Lachner, Kreutzer, and Seyfried; with Mayseder I have had a very long conversation. There is an almost unanimous opinion that I play too softly, or rather, too delicately for the public here. That is to say, they are accustomed to the drum beating of their own Piano *virtuosi*. I am afraid the newspapers will say the same thing, especially as the daughter of one of the editors drums dreadfully; but never mind, if it is to be so, I would much rather they said I played too gently than too roughly.

Count Dietrichstein, one of the personages nearest to the Emperor, came on to the stage yesterday, and had a long talk with me in French, complimented me and requested me to stay longer in Vienna.

The Orchestra execrated my badly written score, and were not at all favourable to me up to the moment of my improvisation; then, in concert with the public, they applauded heartily, which showed their good opinion of me. I do not know yet what the other artists think; but why should they especially be against me? They see that I do not play for pecuniary advantage.

So my first performance, unexpected as it was, has passed off successfully. Hube thinks that one never succeeds in anything by ordinary means and according to preconceived plans, but must trust somewhat to chance. So I trusted to my good fortune and allowed myself to be persuaded to give the concert. If the newspapers cut me up so much that I shall not venture before the world again, I have resolved to become a house painter; that would be as easy as anything else, and I should, at any rate, still be an artist!

I am curious to hear what Herr Elsner will say to all this. Perhaps he disapproves of my playing at all? But I was so besieged on all sides that I had no escape, and I do not seem to have committed a blunder by my performance.

Nidecki* was particularly friendly to me yesterday; he looked through and corrected the orchestral

* Thomas Nidecki, one of the best pupils at the Warsaw Lyceum, was sent to Vienna, in 1822, at the public expense to complete his education. He became bandmaster at the Leopoldstadter Theatre. From 1841 he was bandmaster at the Grand Theatre, in Warsaw, in which City he died in 1852.

parts, and was sincerely pleased at the applause I received. I played on one of Graff's pianos. I am at least four years wiser and more experienced.

You must, indeed, have wondered at my sealing my last letter with a strange seal. I was absent-minded and took the first and best that came to hand.*

Adieu,

Your fondly loving

FREDERIC.

———

Thursday, August 13th, 1829.

If ever I longed to be with you I do so now.

To-day I have become acquainted with Count Lichnowski. He did not know how to praise me enough, he was so delighted with my playing. Würfel took me to him. He was Beethoven's best friend, to whom the great master was much indebted.

Everyone says that I have especially pleased the *noblesse* here. The Schwarzenberg's, Wrbna's, and others were quite enthusiastic about the delicacy and elegance of my execution; in proof of this take Count Dietrichstein's coming on the stage to me. Countess Lichnowski and her daughter, with whom I drank tea to-day, are quite delighted that I am

---

* The seal belonged to the waiter, and bore the word "Madeira."

going to give a second concert on Tuesday. They
invited me to visit them if I passed through Vienna,
on my way to Paris, then they wished to give me
a letter to a certain Countess, sister to Count
Lichnowski. A great deal too much kindness.
Czerny, Schuppanzigh, and Gyrowtez have also
paid me many compliments.

To-day a stranger looked at me in the ante-room,
and, asking Celinski if I was Chopin, rushed up to
me. He spoke of the pleasure he should have in
becoming acquainted with such an artist, and said,
" You really delighted and enchanted me the day
before yesterday." It was the same gentleman who
had sat beside Maciejowski and seemed so delighted
with my improvisation on " Chmiel."

Under no circumstances will I give a third concert;
I only give a second because I am forced to, and I
thought that people might say in Warsaw, " He only
gave *one* concert in Vienna, probably he was not
much liked." To-day I was at the house of one of
the newspaper critics, who is very well disposed
towards me, and is sure to write a favourable
critique. I cannot tell you how kind and pleasant
Würfel is. I shall play gratuitously the second
time also, for the sake of obliging Gallenberg, whose
finances are not very flourishing. (But this is a
secret.) I shall play the Rondo, and then improvise.
For the rest, I am in good health, and eat and drink
well. Vienna pleases me much, and I am not without the society of my countrymen; there is one in

the ballet, who took charge of me at my *débût*, and brought me *eau sucrée*.

Please relate all I write to Elsner, and beg him to pardon me for not writing to him, but my time is really so filled up that I have not a moment to spare. I wish to thank M. Skarbek, who was one of the foremost in persuading me to give a concert; and this is, indeed, the artist's first step in life.

Your ever affectionate

FREDERIC.

Vienna, August 19th, 1829.

If on the first occasion the public were favourable, my reception, yesterday, was still more hearty. I was greeted, when I came on to the stage with three long rounds of applause. The financial manager— whose name I cannot remember—thanked me for the receipts, and said that the house could not have been so full on account of the ballet, for that had been given several times.

The profession praise my Rondo, one and all, from the bandmaster, Lachner, to the piano-tuner. I know I have pleased the ladies and the musicians. Gyrowetz, who sat next Celinski, called, "Bravo," and made a tremendous noise. The only people not satisfied were the out-and-out Germans. Yesterday, one of them, who had just come from the theatre, sat down to eat at the table I was sitting at.

His acquaintances asked him how he liked the performance. "The ballet is pretty," was his answer. "But the concert, what of that?" they asked. Instead of replying he began to talk of something else, from which I conclude that he recognized me, although my back was towards him. I felt bound to relieve him from the restraint of my presence, and went to bed, saying to myself, "The man has not been born yet who does everything right." *

I am glad to be able to say that my popularity increases. As I depart at 9 o'clock this evening, I must spend all the forenoon in farewell visits. Schuppanzigh said, yesterday, that as I was leaving Vienna so quickly, I must come again soon. I answered that I should gladly return for the sake of further improving myself, to which the Baron replied, "that for such a reason I should never need to come, for I had nothing more to learn." This opinion was confirmed by the others. These are, indeed, mere compliments, but one does not listen to them unwillingly. For the future I shall at any rate not be regarded as a student.

Blahetka tells me that what he most wonders at is that I could learn it all in Warsaw. I answered that the greatest donkey must learn something with Messrs. Zwyny and Elsner.

It is very unfortunate for me that I cannot

---

* An old Polish proverb.

confirm what I have told you by sending you the
opinions in the press. I know that the critique is
in the hands of the Editor of the paper to which
I have subscribed, and which Bäuerle * will send
to Warsaw. I expect they waited for my second
performance before giving a notice. This paper
comes out twice a week, Tuesdays and Saturdays,
possibly therefore you may read what is favourable
or the contrary about me before I do.

I have on my side the learned, and those who have
poetic temperaments. We shall have a great deal
to talk over. I would have written of something
quite different, but my head is so full of yesterday
that it is quite impossible to collect my thoughts.
My finances are still in the best order.

I have just paid my farewell visit to Schuppanzigh
and Czerny. Czerny was warmer than any of his
compositions. I have packed up, but must go again
to Haslinger's, and then to the café opposite the
theatre, where I am to meet Gyrowetz, Lachner,

---

* The "Wiener Theater Zeitung," published by Adolph
Bäuerle, from 1828 to 1848, was to every artist an important
and dreaded publication. There were then but few papers
devoted to art matters, and this journal was to be found in the
clubs and coffee-houses of every town in Germany. Whoever
was praised by the "Wiener Theater Zeitung," was a made
man. Bäuerle was the composer also of "Staberl, Staberl's
Hochzeitstag," "Aline, Queen of Golconda, or, Vienna in
another quarter of the world," and "The false Catalini,"
pieces which were performed an immense number of times.

Kreutzer, Seyfried, and others. In two nights and a day we shall be at Prague; the mail coach goes at nine. It will be an agreeable journey with such pleasant companions.

Your FREDERIC.

Prague, Saturday, August 22nd, 1829.

After an affecting parting, which indeed it was, for Fraulein Blahetka * gave me as a souvenir, a copy of her compositions, with her autograph, and united with her father in sending warmest regards to you my good Papa, and to you my dear Mamma, with congratulations to you both on having such a son; young Stein wept, and Schuppanzigh, Gyrowetz, in short all the artists were deeply moved : after this tender farewell, and giving a promise of returning soon, I got into the diligence. Nidecki and two other Poles, who were to start for Trieste in half an hour, accompanied us a little way. One of them, Niegolewski by name, comes from Great Poland, and is travelling with his tutor, or rather, companion, a student from the Warsaw University; we had met and conversed several times in Vienna.

---

* Leopolda Blahetka, born in Vienna, Nov. 15th, 1811, a distinguished pianoforte *virtuoso*, pupil of Czerny and Moscheles. She made several artistic *tournées*, winning everywhere the highest approbation. Her amiability was also much noted.

Countess Hussarzweska (she and her husband are both excellent people) wanted to keep me to dinner when I paid my farewell visit, but I had not time to stay, having to go to Haslinger's. After many hearty wishes for a speedy meeting, Haslinger promised, most solemnly, to bring out my variations in five weeks, that he may have something new to offer the musical world in the autumn. Although a stranger to you, my dear Father, he wished to be kindly remembered.

When we were taking our places in the coach, a young German got in, and, as we were to sit together for two nights and a day, we scraped an acquaintance. He was a merchant from Danzig, knew Pruszaka, Sierakowski, of Waplew, Jaurek, Ernemann, Gresser, and others. He was in Warsaw two years ago, and had now just come from Paris. His name is Normann. He was a very agreeable gentleman and a capital travelling companion. We are in the same hotel with him, and have resolved, when we have seen Prague, to go on together to Teplitz and Dresden. It would be inexcusable to miss seeing Dresden when we are so near, especially as our finances will permit of it, and the journey for four persons is easily managed, and not expensive.

After a good shaking in the coach, we reached Prague at noon, yesterday, and went at once to *table-d'hôte.* Then we called upon Hanka,* to whom

---

* Waclaw Hanka, a celebrated philologist and Slavonic linguist, founder of the reviving Czech national life; born in 1791, died in Prague, 1861.

Maciejowski had a letter of introduction; I regretted afterwards that I had not asked Skarbek to furnish me with one to this famous savant. As we had stayed some time at the Cathedral and Castle we did not find Hanka at home.

The town, viewed from the castle hill, is large and old-fashioned, but handsome in the general; formerly it was an important place.*

Before leaving Vienna I had six letters given me, five from Würfel and one from Blahetka, to Pixis, asking him to show me the Conservatoire here.

They wanted me to play; but I shall only stay three days, and I have no desire to forfeit the renown I won in Vienna. As Paganini even was sharply criticised, I shall take care not to perform in this place. The five letters from Würfel are to the Theatre director, the bandmaster, and other musical celebrities. I shall deliver the letters, for he asked me to very earnestly; but I will not perform. The excellent Würfel has also given me a letter to Klengel,† in Dresden.

---

* Especially in the time of Otto the Great the last independent King of Bohemia, who was conquered by Rudolph of Habsburgh, and died on the field of March. From 1790 to 1848 the Royal Theatre at Prague was one of the best and most celebrated in Germany.

† August Alexander Klengel, one of the most celebrated pianoforte *virtuosi*, born January 27th, 1783, was a pupil of Clementi. The pianoforte studies which he wrote are unsurpassed. He composed besides ninety-six Canons and Fugues In 1819 he went as organist to the Royal Catholic Church in Dresden, and died there in 1852.

I must now conclude, as it is quite time to go to Hanka's. I shall introduce myself as godson of Count Skarbek, and I hope that no further recom- mendation will be necessary.

Your FREDERIC.

Dresden, August 26th, 1829.

I am merry and well. When I was in Vienna, a week ago, I did not dream I should be in Dresden to-day. Our stay at Prague was very short, but not without profit. Herr Hanka was very pleased to receive news from Skarbek. Like all visitors to the Prague Museum who have received any special atten- tion from Herr Hanka, we had to write our names in a book kept for the purpose; we found among others the names of Brodzinski, Mocawski,* &c. Each of us wrote whatever occurred to him in poetry or prose. What could I, a musician, write that would be worth reading? The thought happily struck Maciejowski to write four strophes for a Mazurka, and I set them to music; so I think we have both immortalized ourselves in the most characteristic manner.

Hanka was delighted with this idea, for the Mazourka contained a reference to him and to his efforts for the elevation of the Slavs. He has given

----

* Two famous Polish poets.

me several views of Prague for Skarbek. I cannot possibly tell you by letter all that Herr Hanka showed us. I must describe, verbally, the lovely views, the majestic cathedral, with the figure of St. John, in silver, the beautiful chapel of St. Wencelaus, inlaid with amethysts and other precious stones, and many other things.

I am indebted to Blahetka's and Würfel's letters for the friendly reception which I had from Pixis. He gave up his lessons, kept me at his house, and asked me about all sorts of things. I noticed Klengel's visiting card on his table, and asked if it belonged to a relative of the famous Klengel, of Dresden. "Klengel himself is here," replied Pixis; "he called while I was out."

I was delighted at the prospect of becoming acquainted with this artist, to whom I had letters from Wurfel. I spoke to Pixis about it, and he invited me to come in the afternoon, if I wished to meet Klengel, as he was expected then. We met by accident on the steps of Pixis's house, and effected our first acquaintance there. I listened to his fugues for more than two hours; I did not play, as I was not asked. Klengel's playing pleased me, but, to speak candidly, I had expected something still better. (I pray you not to mention this to anyone.) He gave me an introductory letter with the following address: "Al ornatissimo Signore Cavaliere Morlacchi, primo Maestro della Capella Reale;" in which he begs this gentleman to make me acquainted

F

with the whole musical world of Dresden, and in particular to present me to Fräulein Pechwell. This lady is a pupil of Klengel's and, in his opinion, the first pianist in Dresden. He was extremely affable towards me. Before his departure—he is going to Vienna and Italy—I spent a couple of hours with him, and our conversation never flagged. This has been a very agreeable acquaintanceship, and I value it more highly than Czerny's; but not a word of this either, my dear ones.

The three delightful days in Prague were over before we were aware.

I am, as you know, very absent-minded, and on the day we left rushed suddenly into a strange room without knowing. "Good morning," said a cheerful voice. "I beg your pardon, I mistook the the number," I answered, and ran away as fast as possible. We left Prague at noon in a private carriage, and arrived at Teplitz towards evening. The next day I found in the list at the Baths Ludwig Lempicki's name; I immediately went to call on him. He was very glad to see me, and told me there were several Poles here; among others he mentioned old Pruszack, Joseph Köhler, and Kretkowski, from Kamiona. Lempicki told me that they generally all dined together in the "German hall," but that to-day he was invited to Prince Clary's Castle. This Prince belongs to one of the most distinguished of the Austrian princely families. He is very wealthy, and owns the town

of Teplitz. Princess Clary, née Countess Chotek *
is sister of the present Oberstburggraf of Bohemia.
Lempicki said he was quite at home in Prince
Clary's house, and would introduce me there in
the evening when the Princess always gave recep-
tions; he would mention my name to them at
dinner. Having no engagement for the evening,
I accepted the proposal with pleasure.

We have seen all that is worth seeing here, and
have also been to Dux, the residence of the Count
Waldsteins. We were shown the halberd with
which Albrecht Waldstein (or Wallenstein) was
stabbed, a piece of his scull, and other relics.
In the evening, instead of going to the theatre,
I dressed and went with Lempicki to the Castle.
I put on my white gloves which had already done
duty at the Vienna concert. The company was
not numerous, but very select: an Austrian prince;
an Austrian general, whose name I forget; an
English naval captain; two or three elegant dandies
(Austrian princes or counts, I believe); and the
Saxon General von Leiser, who bore the uncommon
decoration of a scar on his face.

I talked most to Prince Clary. After tea Countess
Chotek, mother of the Princess, asked me to play.

---

* Princess Aloysia von Clary was an extremely amiable
lady. She was an excellent pianist, and to rare culture united
true goodness of heart. Artists and poets met with the most
cordial reception in her hospitable house, and to extreme old
age the Princess took a warm interest in all artistic matters.

The instrument was a good one, by Graff. I took my seat at the piano, and asked the company to give me a theme for improvisation. The ladies, who had established themselves at a table, immediately whispered to each other " un thème, un thème." Three pretty young princesses, after some consultation, referred to a Herr Fritsche,* tutor to Prince Clary's only son, and he suggested the chief theme in Rossini's " Moses," which was unanimously approved of. I improvised, I suppose with some success, for General von Leiser had a long talk with me afterwards. When he heard I was going to Dresden, he at once wrote the following to Baron von Friesen.

" Monsieur Frédéric Chopin est recommandé de la part du General Leiser a Monsieur le Baron de Friesen, Maître de Cérémonie de S. M. le roi de Saxe, pour lui être utile pendant son séjour à Dresde, et de lui procurer la connaissance de plusieurs des premièrs artistes."

Below was written in German: " Herr Chopin is one of the best pianists I have heard." I copied this literally for you, my dearests, from the general's pencil letter.

I had to play four times. The Prince and Princess asked me to prolong my stay at Teplitz, and dine with them the next day. Lempicki offered to accompany me to Warsaw, if I remained a

---

* Composer of several short comedies which were performed successfully in Dresden and Vienna, between the years 1836 and 1848.

day or two here, but I could not hear of being separated from my companions, so, with many thanks, I declined both proposals.

We left yesterday morning, at 5 o'clock, in a carriage, for which we paid two Thalers, and arrived at Dresden at four in the afternoon, when we met Lewinski and Lebecki. Everything has happened very fortunately for me throughout the journey. The first part of " Faust ", is to be given to-day, and Klengel tells me that the Italian opera will be on Saturday.

This letter was begun last night. Now I must dress for calling on Baron von Friesen and Morlacchi, so have no time to spare. We intend leaving in a week, but, weather permitting, not without seeing the Saxon Switzerland. We hope to spend a few days in Breslau, and go direct home from there. I am longing so much to see you again, my dear parents, that I do not at all care to go to Wiesio-lowski's first. Oh, how many stories and adventures I shall have to relate, and each more interesting than the last.

P.S.—Baron von Friesen, maître dé cérémonie, received me very kindly. He asked me where I was staying, and regretted that the Chamberlain, who was also director of the royal band, was not at Dresden just now, but he would find out who was his deputy, and do all he could to show me something worth seeing during my short sojourn. Whereupon many bows and stammered thanks on

my part.　My next letter, from Breslau, will tell you
the rest.*　I have seen the world-renowned gallery,
the fruit show, the gardens, have paid some visits,
and am now going to the theatre.　Enough, I hope,
for one day.

SECOND POSTCRIPT.—It is night.　Just returned
from the theatre, where I saw " Faust." †　The rush
was so great that we had to be in the *queue*, outside
the office, before five o'clock, to get a ticket at all.
The performance began at six, and lasted till
eleven o'clock.　Devrient, ‡ whom I saw in Berlin,
acted *Faust*.　A fearful but magnificent conception.
Portions of Spohr's Opera, " Faust," were performed
as Entr'actes.　Goethe's eightieth birthday was
celebrated to-day.　Now I am off to bed,　I expect
Morlacchi early to-morrow, and shall go with him
to Fräulein Pechwell's, that is, he will come
with me.

Good night,

Your FREDERIC.

---

* I have not found any letters from Breslau.　He probably
hurried on as fast as he could, to give his news in person.

† The first part of Goethe's " Faust " was performed for the
first time, that evening, in Dresden.　Louis Tieck had made
the necessary curtailments.

‡ Charles Devrient, eldest of the three brothers, and nephew
of the great Louis Devrient.

CHAPTER VI.

INFLUENCE OF THE LAST JOURNEY ON CHOPIN.
LETTERS TO TITUS WOYCIECHOWSKI. FAREWELL
CONCERT IN WARSAW.
CHOPIN LEAVES HIS NATIVE CITY.

THE innocent youthful gaiety which accompanied
Chopin on his journey was his faithful companion for some time to come. The brilliant success
of his two performances in Vienna assured him that
he really had talent, and that his parents had not
done wrong in allowing him to dedicate himself
wholly to art.

He returned from his second journey with wider
views and riper judgment. He left off drawing
caricatures, with which, in boyish mischief, he had
often amused himself in Berlin. He felt, with
intense delight, that the wings of his genius were
bearing him higher than they did a year ago. With
his inborn modesty he was surprised that great
musicians should marvel at his playing; he had,
indeed, already the courage to defend his opinions
when they differed from those of other musicians;

but he always spoke with a certain reserve and courtesy, which prevented him from giving offence, nor did he forget to pay the respect which the young man owes to the elder. "That Vienna would lose much if he went away without letting people hear him," was incomprehensible to the modest youth not yet fully conscious of his talents.

It is characteristic of Chopin that he always began his letters in a clear elegant hand; but, as if overpowered by the rush of thought and feeling, the writing, as he proceeded, grew larger and more hurried. His Polish letters are pithy and natural, and often contain surprisingly original thoughts. A great deal cannot be transcribed into German, although this language bears the palm for the best translations.

Frederic's humorous nature was often displayed in the address of a letter. For example, he sent one to his father directed " To the Right Hon. N. Chopin, Professor in Warsaw, and to the dear parents of the son who is in Dresden." He would often call his sisters "my children" (mojo dzieci), out of tenderness, and add some playful affectionate expressions. He never forgot to send remembrances to his much-honoured teachers, Zwyny and Elsner, nor to gladden his fellow collegians and intimate friends by kind words as reminders of himself.

It has become the custom with most of the writers on Chopin to dilate on his weak and exhausted health. The grossest exaggerations have been current on this point, and, as is nearly always the case, more credence has been given to the exaggerations than to the truth. Goethe says truly, " People believe the truth so little because it is so simple."

It has been said of Chopin that he suffered from his earliest years from an incurable malady which might have caused death at any moment. This may have been the reason why Liszt describes him as very sickly when only a youth of fifteen or sixteen ; among other things about him he says :

" * * * * Chopin was more like one of those ideal creations with which the poetry of the middle ages adorned the Christian temples : a beautiful angel, with a form pure and slight as a young god of Olympus, with a face like that of a majestic woman filled with a divine sorrow, and, as the crown of all, an expression at the same time tender and severe, chaste and impassioned.

" He daily accustomed himself to think that the hour of his death was near, and, under the influence of this feeling, he accepted the careful attentions of a friend, from whom he concealed how short a time, he believed, remained for him on earth. He possessed great physical courage, and, if he did not accept with the heroic care-lessness of youth the idea of his approaching end, he at least cherished the expectation of it with a kind of bitter pleasure."

These remarks are not applicable to that period of Chopin's life, for they are not in accordance with the facts. Chopin neither looked like "a beautiful

angel," "a majestic woman filled with a divine
sorrow," nor "a young god from Olympus;" just as
little did he imagine daily "that the hour of his
death was near." On the contrary, his cheerful
letters, pervaded with the joy of youth, showed that
Frederic had as good health as any other young
man of his age. When travelling he saw all that
was worth seeing, gave two concerts within a week,
paid several visits, was present at long performances
at the theatre, and wrote a great many letters
besides. Undeniably, Chopin had a delicate constitution, but he was healthy, and strong enough to
bear the fatigue of travelling in a diligence.

It was not until ten years later that he was
threatened with the illness brought on by the excitement of Paris life. And if Frederic had been
sickly, would his parents have permitted their only,
tenderly loved son to travel abroad? Would they
have consented to an absence of two years—which
followed the earlier journeys—if the young artist
had been troubled with a dangerous malady? Only
in the last years of his life his physical strength was
often greatly exhausted, in consequence of the rapid
strides of the disease which caused his early death.

Chopin's playmate and schoolfellow, Wilhelm von
Kolberg, who is still living in Warsaw, affirms that
till manhood, Chopin was only ill once, and then
from a cold. It is true that after the manner of
loving womanly hearts, mother and sisters very
much petted their dear Frederic. There was no

lack of exhortations to "wrap up carefully in cold
damp weather;" he laughed good-humouredly at the
instructions, but followed them like an obedient son.

Theıe were moments when, buried in thought,
Frederıc paıd little heed to the outer world, and
avoided even his best friends. These were times of
communion with hıs muse, and he would suffer the
interventıon of no thırd person.

In a general way he was fond of pleasure, and
delighted to share it wıth his parents, famıly and
friends. He never marred anyone's enjoyment. If
he were among company who wished to dance, he
would sit down to the piano without being pressed
and play the most charmıng Mazurkas and other
dances. If a bad player were at the piano, he would
politely and pleasantly put himself in hıs place. In
after years also, when he lived in Paris and had
acquıred a European reputation, he was always
willing, in the kindest manner, to delight a Polish
famıly with some natıonal dances. As a player he
was as indefatigable as the dancers, who ın their
enthusıasm often did not know how to stop.

Like all intelligent young men, Frederıc returned
from his travels wıth a wider knowledge of human
nature. He perceıved that the artists, whose ac-
quaıntance he had lately made, were not all so
amiable and frce from envy as he had imagıned; he,
therefore, clung the closer to the more noble-minded
among his compeers, for whom he retaıned through
life a friendly recollection.

Unfortunately, he did not fail to meet with bitter disappointments in later years.

The artists in Vienna looked upon Chopin as a young man with a thorough and most refined musical education, who was not puffed up with vanity, and had no thought of settling in the Imperial city. They were, therefore, favourably disposed towards him, and willingly lent their assistance.

Like every true artist and poet, Chopin was tormented with doubts as to the extent and range of his genius. Some, indeed, who heard him at the concerts which he gave in Vienna, said that his playing was not powerful enough; but with regard to his compositions there was but one opinion. Real connoisseurs of pianoforte playing, truly musical souls, knew how to value the smoothness, certainty, and elegance of his style. The wonderful penetrating and melancholy expression peculiar to Chopin's playing, found a response in all poetical minds. He was pre-eminently the pianist for poets, and could not be exalted too highly above the mass, who only desire technical skill and noise; the musicians were especially interested by the character and originality of his compositions. To complete the story of his Vienna experiences, I give two letters to his most intimate friend Woyciechowski.

Warsaw, September 12th, 1829.

DEAREST TITUS,

You would not have heard from me, if I had not met Vicentius Skarbek, and thereby been reminded that you would be in Warsaw by the end of this month. I hoped that I should have been able to tell you personally of my GREAT JOURNEY, for truly and sincerely I should only be too glad to have a chat with you. But as this is unfortunately impossible, let me tell you, dear, that I have been to Cracow, Vienna, Prague, Dresden and Breslau.

We passed the first week at Cracow in taking walks, and visiting the neighbourhood. Ojcow is very beautiful; but I shall not say anything, for although you were not there, you know all about it from Tanska's accurate descriptions. I had good company on my way to Vienna; if Cracow made so many demands upon me that I could not find a few moments to think of you and my family, Vienna so utterly stupefied and infatuated me, that, although a fortnight passed without my receiving a letter from home, I felt no longing for my friends. Just imagine my playing twice in the Royal and Imperial Theatre in so short a time. This is how it came about: my publisher Haslinger represented to me that it would be of advantage to my compositions if I were to appear in Vienna; that my name was as yet unknown, and my music difficult both to play and understand.

I did not yet think of it seriously, and replied:

"That I had not played a note for a fortnight, and so was not prepared to present myself before a select and critical public." In the meantime Count Gallenberg, who writes pretty ballets, and is manager of the Vienna theatre, came in. Haslinger introduced me to him as a coward, afraid of appearing in public. The Count very obligingly placed the theatre at my disposal, but I was shrewd enough to decline, with thanks. The next day Würfel came in, and urged me not to bring disgrace on my parents, Elsner, and myself by neglecting the opportunity of performing in Vienna.

As soon as I had yielded to all this pressure, Würfel at once undertook the necessary preparations. The next morning bills announced my concert. It was impossible, therefore, to retreat, although I did not know how or what I should play. Three manufacturers proposed to send me pianos, but, owing to the narrow limits of my lodgings, I was obliged to refuse their offers. What would have been the use either of my practising a great deal two days before the concert?

In one day I made the acquaintance of all the great artists in Vienna, among them Mayseder, Gyrowetz, Lachner, Kreutzer, Schuppanzigh, &c.

The members of the orchestra looked sourly at me during the rehearsal; they were particularly vexed at my making my *début* with new compositions. Then I began the Variations dedicated to you, which were to come after the Rondo Cracovienne. The

Variations were a success, but the Rondo, owing to the way in which it was written, went so badly that we were obliged to commence from the beginning twice. I ought to have put the pauses below instead of above. Enough; the gentlemen made such wry faces that I felt very much inclined to announce myself ill in the evening.

Demmar, the manager, noticed the ill-temper of the orchestra, who do not like Würfel. The latter wished to conduct himself, but the orchestra declined (I don't know why) to play under his lead. Herr Demmar advised me to improvise, at which proposal the orchestra stared. I was so much irritated by what had happened that I consented in despair; and who knows whether my miserable mood and strange humour were not the cause of the great success I achieved?

The presence of the Viennese public did not excite me at all, and I sat down, very calmly, to a wonderful instrument of Graff's, the best, perhaps, then in Vienna. Beside me sat a young man, covered with rouge, who had turned over for me in the Variations, and plumed himself on having rendered the same service to Moscheles, Hummel, and Herz. I played, as you may imagine, in a desperate mood; the Variations, nevertheless, made such an effect that I was encored enthusiastically. Fräulein Veltheim sang very beautifully. As to my Improvisation I only know that it was followed by a storm of applause and many recalls.

The Vienna newspapers were lavish in their praise. By universal desire I played again a week after, congratulating myself that no one could say now that I was only able to appear once. I was especially pleased with the performance of the Rondo, because Gyrowetz, Lachner, and other masters, and even the orchestra were so delighted—forgive me for saying so—that they recalled me twice. I was obliged to repeat the Variations (at the special request of the ladies) ; Haslinger, too, was so pleased with them that he is going to bring them out in *Odeon ;* a great honour for me, is it not ?

Lichnowski, one of Beethoven's friends, wished to lend me his piano for the concert (this is, indeed, something), as it seemed to him that mine was too weak. But this was on account of my style of playing, which pleased the ladies so much ; especially Fräulein Blahetka. It might be that she is favourably disposed towards me (by the way, she is not yet twenty, a lovely and intelligent girl). At my departure she honoured me by a composition, with an inscription in her own handwriting.

The *Wiener Zeitung* said, in a notice of the second concert, " This is a young man who knows how to please by entirely original means. His style differs totally from that of the ordinary concert giver. I hope this is satisfactory, especially as the article concludes, " Herr Chopin to-day again received the most unanimous applause." Pardon me for writing such an opinion of myself, but I do so because it pleases me more than any amount of praise in the *Warsaw Courier*.

I became quite intimate with Czerny, and often played with him on two pianos. He is a good-natured man, but nothing more. Klengel, whom I saw at Pixis's, in Prague, I like best of all my artistic acquaintances. He played his fugues to me (one might call them a continuation of Bach's, there are forty-eight, and as many canons.) What a contrast to Czerny! Klengel gave me a letter of introduction to Morlacchi, in Dresden. We visited the Saxon Switzerland, so rich in natural beauties, and the magnificent picture gallery; but the Italian Opera had to be given up before my very eyes. I was, unfortunately, obliged to leave the day on which "Crociato in Egitto" was to be performed. My only consolation was that I had already heard it in Vienna.

Frau Pruszak, and her two children, Alexandrine and Constantin, are in Dresden. I met them the day I left. What a pleasure! They called out, "Pan Frycek, Pan Frycek;"* it was so charming that I should certainly have stayed but for my companions. Herr Pruszak I met at Teplitz. Teplitz is a wonderfully beautiful place. I was only there a day, but went to a soirée at Prince Clary's.

I have been too much absorbed in my writing to

* The Polish for Frederic.

be able to stop. I affectionately embrace you, and kiss your lips, if you allow me.

Your FREDERIC.

Warsaw, October 3rd, 1829.

DEAREST TITUS,

You write that you have read something about my concerts in two newspapers; if they were Warsaw papers, you could certainly not have been gratified, for not only is their translation bad, but they have taken the trouble to distort, to my disparagement, the comments of the Viennese critics. The Vienna *Sammler* and the *Zeitschrift für Literatur,* from which Hube brought me the extracts, made the most flattering criticisms on my playing and compositions (pardon me for writing this to you), and called me, in conclusion, " An independent *virtuoso,* full of delicacy and the deepest feeling." * If such extracts had fallen into your hands I should have no occasion to be ashamed.

You will learn from me bye and bye what I think of doing this winter. In no case shall I remain in Warsaw; where fate will lead me I do not yet know. Prince and Princess Radziwill have, in the most polite manner, invited me to Berlin, and offered me

---

* Edward Hanslick, in his book, " History of Concerts in Vienna," uses the same words as the *Sammler* does about Chopin.

appartments in their palace; but of what use would this be? I have begun so much work that it would seem the wisest course for me to remain here. I have also promised to return to Vienna, and a Vienna paper openly declared that a sojourn in the Imperial city would be very advantageous to me, and 'have the best influence on my career.

You will, perhaps, think so too; but do not imagine that I am thinking about Fraulein Blahetka, whom I mentioned in my letter. I have already—to my misfortune, perhaps—found my ideal, which I sincerely and loyally worship. Half a year has passed without exchanging a syllable with her of whom I dream every night. While thinking of this lovely being I composed the Adagio in my new Concerto,* and early this morning the Waltz, which I send you. Notice the passage marked +, nobody knows of it but yourself. How glad I should be if I could play my newest compositions to you, my dear friend. In the fifth bar of the Trio, the melody in the bass must rise to the higher E flat in the violin cleff, which, however, I need not tell you, for you will feel it for yourself.

I have no other news to send than that every Friday there is music at Kessler's. Yesterday they played, among other things, Spohr's Octett, a wonderful work. I go to Brzezina's † every day; he has

---

* E minor Concerto op. 11.
† Book and Music Seller, in Warsaw.

nothing new but Pixis's Concerto which made no
great impression on me; the Rondo seems the best
part of it. You cannot imagine how dull Warsaw
looks. If it were not for the happiness I find with
my family I could not live here.

Oh, how miserable it is to have no one to share
your sorrows and joys, and, when your heart is
heavy, to have no soul to whom you can pour out
your woes. You know very well what I mean.
How often do I communicate to my piano all that
I would confide to you.

My friend, you must change into a delightful
reality my dream of travelling with you abroad. I
do not know what I should do for joy. But, alas,
our ways lie wide apart.

I hope to go to Italy, from Vienna, for my further
improvement, and next winter I am to meet Hube
in Paris; but everything may be altered, as my kind
father would like me to go to Berlin, for which, to
say the truth, I have no great desire. If, as I trust, I
go to Vienna, I shall, perhaps, choose the way through
Dresden and Prague, to visit Klengel again; also
the famous picture gallery and the Conservatoire.

I must now leave off, or I shall only weary you
with my dry news, and I do not want to do that.
If you would only write me a few lines, it would give
me pleasure for several weeks. Forgive me for
sending you the Waltz, which will make you angry
with me in the end. My intention is to please you.

Your FREDERIC.

The favourable critiques in the Vienna newspapers of Chopin's playing awakened universal interest in Warsaw, and caused his father to take counsel with Elsner and other friends about Frederic's further training.   All agreed on sending the young artist for a longer sojourn abroad.   Warsaw offered, indeed, little artistic stimulus to Chopin's extraordinary abilities; he passed there for a perfect artist.   His compositions, published in Warsaw, are among the best he ever wrote, and if his creative talent grew and matured in later years, his early works bear the true Chopin stamp.

Elsner's advice was that Chopin should go to Italy first, then to Paris, and so be away two years in all.   From letters to his friend, Titus Woyciechowski, who now resides at his estate Poturzyn, in Poland, and who very kindly furnished these letters, we learn from Frederic himself how he passed the next few years.   It is most fortunate for us that his most intimate friend has religiously preserved, as sacred memorials, every line of the talented artist.

Warsaw, October 20th, 1829.

MY DEAREST TITUS,

You won't know how to make out why such a writing mania has suddenly seized me, and how it is that, in so short a time, I send you a third letter.

I start at seven this evening, *per diligence*, for Wiesiowlowski's, in Posen, and so write to you beforehand, not knowing how long I shall stay there, though I have only got a passport for a month. My idea is to return in about a fortnight. The object of my journey is to see Prince Radziwill, who is living at his estate not far from Kalitz. He wishes me to go to Berlin, and live as a guest in his house, &c.; but I cannot see that it would be of any real, that is to say, artistic use. " Mit grossen Herren ist nicht gut Kirschen essen."

My good father will not believe that these invita‧ tions are merely *des belles paroles*.

Forgive me if I repeat myself. I easily forget what I have written, and often fancy I am giving you news which is really stale.

Kessler gives a musical soirée every Friday; nearly all the artists here meet together, and play whatever is brought forward, *prima vista;* so, for example, there were performed, last Friday: Concerto in C sharp minor, by Ries, with quartet accompaniment; then Trio in E major, by Hummel; Beethoven's last Trio, which I thought magnificent and impressive; also a Quartet, by Prince Louis Ferdinand of Prussia, *alias* Dussek; * and singing to conclude with.

Elsner has praised my Concerto Adagio. He says

---

* Chopin says what he may have heard reported, for it is well known that the world rarely credits the nobly born with artistic talent. Prince Louis Ferdinand was, indeed, Dussek's pupil, but he was not, therefore, helped in his compositions by

there is something new in it.   As for the Rondo I do
not want any opinion on that at present, for I am
not satisfied with it myself.   I wonder whether I
shall finish it when I return.

Thank you very much for your letter, which
pleased me exceedingly.   You have the happy gift
of cheering and delighting one.   You cannot imagine
how despondent I was in the morning, and how my
spirits rose when I received your letter.   I embrace
you warmly.   Many write this at the end of their
letters and scarcely think about it ; but you know,
dearest friend, that I do it sincerely, as truly as I
am called " Fritz."   I have composed a Study in my
style ; when we meet again I will play it to you.

Your faithful

FREDERIC.

Warsaw, Sunday, November 14th, 1829.

DEAREST TITUS,

I received your last letter at Radziwill's, at
Antonin.   I was there a week, and you cannot think
how quickly and pleasantly the time passed.   I

---

his teacher.   Prince Ferdinand—called Louis Ferdinand in
history, and on the title pages of his compositions—was of an
inventive nature, and what works he has left are really the
produce of his own brain.   Full of patriotism and courage, he
took part in the war and fell at Saalfield, October 13th, 1806.

travelled back by the last Post, and had great trouble to get away. As for myself I could have stayed there till I was driven away, but my occupations, and, above all, my concerto, which still impatiently awaits its *Finale*, forced me to quit Paradise.

My dear Titus, there were three daughters of Eve there; the young princesses, extremely amiable, musical, and kind-hearted; and the Princess, their mother, who knows quite well that the value of a man does not depend on his descent, is so lady-like and amiable towards everyone that it is impossible not to honour her.

You know what a lover of music the Prince is. He showed me his " Faust," and I found much that is really beautiful in it; some parts, indeed, show considerable intellectual power. Between ourselves, I certainly should not have accredited a Stadtholder with such music. I was struck, among other things, by the scene where Mephistopheles allures Margaret to the window, by playing the guitar and singing outside her house, while a Chorale is heard at the same time in the neighbouring church. This is sure to produce a great sensation. I only mention this to give you an idea of his style. He is also a great admirer of Gluck. In the drama, he only gives importance to music in so far as it depicts the situation or the feelings, therefore the Overture has no conclusion, but leads directly to the introduction. The orchestra is always invisible, placed behind the stage,* so as not to distract the attention by such externals as the conducting, the movements of the musicians, &c.

I wrote an " Alla Polacca," with 'cello accompaniment during my visit to Prince Radziwill. It is nothing more than a brilliant drawing-room piece—suitable for the ladies. I should like Princess Wanda to practice it. I am supposed to have given her lessons. She is a beautiful girl of seventeen, and it was charming to direct her delicate fingers. But, joking apart, she has real musical feeling, and does not need to be told when to play *crescendo, piano,* or *pianissimo.* Princess Elise was so much interested in my Polonaise (F minor) that I could not refuse to send for it. Please let me have it by return of post. I did not wish to be thought impolite, but I should not like to write it out of my head again, my dearest, for I should, perhaps, make it very different from the original. You can picture to yourself the character of the Princess from her having me play the Polonaise to her every day. The Trio in A flat major always pleases her particularly.† She wishes me much to go to Berlin in May, so nothing stands in the way of my going to Vienna in the Winter.

---

* One thinks involuntarily of the Orchestra at the Bayreuth Festival, in 1876. Yes, yes, " Original fahr' him in deiner Pracht."—*Goethe.*

† This polonaise appears as op. 71 in the collection of posthumous works.

It does not seem likely that I shall get off before December. Papa's birthday is on the sixth, which I shall, in any case, keep with him. I do not think of starting till the middle of December. I hope also to see you again.

You would not believe what a blank I feel in Warsaw just now. I have no one to whom I can speak a couple of really confidential words. You want one of my portraits. I certainly would have sent it you if I could have stolen one from Princess Elise, who has two in her album, which, I am assured are very faithful likenesses; but you, my dearest, need no picture of me. Believe me, I am always with you and will never forget you to the end of my life.

I remind you once more of the Polonaise ; please send it by return. I have written some studies ; I should play them well in your presence. Last Saturday, Kessler played Hummel's E major Concerto, at the Ressource. Next Saturday, perhaps, I shall play ; I shall choose the Variations dedicated to you.

Your faithful

FREDERIC.

————

Warsaw, March 27th, 1830.

I never missed you so much as now. I have no one to whom I can pour out my heart. A single look from you, after the concert, would be more to me than the praise of all the critics here. Immediately on the receipt of your letter, I wanted to describe my first concert to you ; but I was so distracted and busy with preparations for the second, which took place on Monday, that I was not capable of collecting my thoughts. I am not, indeed, in a much better mood to-day, but I cannot delay the sending of this letter any longer, for the post goes, and who knows when my mind will be at rest again ?

The first concert, for which three days before there was neither box nor stall to be had, did not, on the whole, make the impression I had expected. The first Allegro of the F. minor concerto (not intelligible to everyone) was indeed rewarded with a bravo, but this was, I think, because the public wished to show that it knew how to understand and appreciate earnest music. In every country there are plenty of people who readily assume the airs of connoisseurs. The Adagio and Rondo made a great effect and were followed by the heartiest applause and shouts of bravo. But the Potpurri on Polish songs * completely missed its mark. They applauded indeed, but, evidently, only to show the player they were not wearied with him.

Kurpinski † thought he discovered fresh beauties

---

* Grand Fantasia on Polish airs, op. 13.

† Charles Kurpinski, bandmaster, and composer of several national operas, was born in 1785, and died in 1857, in Warsaw.

in my concerto that evening. Ernemann was entirely satisfied. Elsner regretted that my piano was not stronger, the bass being, as he thought, not heard clearly enough.

Those sitting in the gallery or standing in the orchestra appear to have been most satisfied; there were complaints in the pit of the playing being too soft. I should very much like to know the gossip about me at " Kopciuszek." * In consequence of the remarks in the pit, Mochnacki, after highly praising me—especially for the Adagio in the *Polish Courier*—advised me, for the future, to use more power and energy. I knew quite well where this power lay, so at the second concert I did not play on my own but on a Vienna instrument. This time the audience, again very large, were perfectly content. The applause knew no bounds, and I was assured that every note rang out like a a bell, and that I played much more finely than before. When I appeared, in reply to a recall, they called out " give another concert." The Cracovienne produced a tremendous sensation ; there were four rounds of applause. Kurpinski regretted that I had not played the Polish Fantasia on the Vienna piano, a remark which Grzymala repeated the other day in the *Polish Courier*. Elsner says I could not be properly judged of until after the second concert.

---

* A coffee-house frequented by most of the *literati;* called in German " Aschenbrodel."

I confess, candidly, that I would rather have played on my own instrument. The Vienna piano was generally regarded as more appropriate to the size of the building.

You know what the programme of the first concert was.* The second began with a Symphony by Nowakowski † (par complaisance) followed by a repetition of the first Allegro of my Concerto. Then the Theatre Concert-master, Bulawski, played an Air Varié, by Beriot, and I, my Allegro and Rondo again. The second part commenced with the Rondo Cracovienne. Meier sang an air from Soliva's opera, " Helene and Malvina," and, in conclusion, I improvised on the Volkslied " W—miescie dziwne obyczaje," (there are strange customs in the town)

---

* The following programme was performed in the Warsaw Theatre, March 17th, 1830.

First Part.

1.—Overture to the Opera " Leszek Bialy," by Elsner.
2.—Allegro from the F minor Concerto, composed and played by Herr F. Chopin.
3.—Divertissement for Horn, composed and played by Herr Gorner.
4.—Adagio and Rondo, from F minor Concerto, composed and played by Herr Chopin.

Second Part.

1.—Overture to the Opera, " Cecilia Piaseczynska," by Kurpinski.
2 —Variations by Paer, sung by Madame Meier.
3.—Pot-pourri on national songs, by Chopin.

† A fellow student of Chopin's, born 1800, died in Warsaw 1865.

which very much pleased the people in the first rows. To be candid I must say that I did not improvise as I had intended, but, perhaps, that would not have been so well suited to the audience. I wonder that the Adagio pleased so generally ; from all I hear, it is with reference to this that the most flattering observations have been made. You must have read the newspapers, and you will see that the public were very pleased with me.

A poem, addressed to me, and a large bouquet were sent to my house. Mazurkas and Waltzes are being arranged on the principal themes from my Concerto. Brzezina asked for my likeness, but I declined giving it. This would be too much all at once, besides I do not like the prospect of butter being wrapped up in the paper on which I am pourtrayed, as was the case with Lelewel's portrait.

Wishes are expressed on all sides that I should give a third concert, but I have no desire to do so. You would not believe the excitement one has to go through for some days before the performance. I hope to finish the first Allegro of the second Concerto before the vacation, so I shall wait, at any rate, till after Easter, although I am convinced that I should have a larger audience than ever this time ; for the " haute volée " have hardly heard me at all yet. At the last concert a stentorian voice called out from the pit, " Play at the Town Hall," but I doubt whether I shall follow this advice ; if I play again, it will be in the theatre. It is not a question of receipts with me, for the Theatre did not bring me in much. (The cashier, to whom everything was left, did as he liked.)   From both concerts, after all expenses had been deducted, I did not receive quite 5,000 gulden,* although Dmuszewski, editor of the *Warsaw Courier*, stated that no concert had been so crowded as mine.   Besides, the Town Hall, where the anxieties and arrangements would be many, would not please everyone.   Dobrzynski † is vexed with me for not performing his symphony.   Frau W. took it amiss that I did not reserve a box for her, &c., &c.

I close this letter unwillingly, because I feel as if I had not told you anything interesting yet.   I have reserved all for the desert which is nothing more than a warm embrace.

Your FREDERIC.

Warsaw, May 15th, 1830.

You will certainly have wondered that Fritz did not answer your letter by return of post; but as I could not immediately give the information you asked for I delayed writing till to-day.

Now listen, my dearest, Henrietta Sonntag is

---

* About 850 Thalers.

† Felix Ignaz Dobrzynski, pianist and composer, born 1807, died in Warsaw, 1865.

coming to Warsaw in June, or, perhaps, at the end of May. I am sure you will not neglect the opportunity of hearing her. Oh, how thankful I am for it. She must be in Danzig now, and from there she comes to us. We have several concerts in prospect. Little Worlitzer, pianist to the King of Prussia, has already been here a fortnight. He plays very finely, and being of Jewish descent, has many natural gifts. He has been with me; he is just sixteen; some of the things he played at our house went famously. His best performance is Moscheles's Variations on the Alexander March. He really plays those excellently. You would like his style and manner of playing, although—this to you only—he still lacks much to deserve his title of Chamber *Virtuoso*. There is also a French pianist here, Monsieur Standt. He intended giving a concert, but seems lately to have relinquished the idea.

It is an agreeable piece of musical news that Herr Blahetka, father of the *pianiste* in Vienna, will, if I advise him, come here, when the Diet meets, and give some concerts. But my position is a difficult one; the man wants to make money, and if it happens that his hopes are not fulfilled, he will be angry with me. I answered immediately that I had often been asked whether he would not come, and that many musicians and lovers of music would be glad to hear his daughter; but I did not conceal from him that Sonntag would be here, that Lipinski was coming, that we have only one theatre, and that the expenses of a concert amount to at least 100 thalers. He cannot say now that I did not properly inform him of the state of things. It is very possible that he will come. I should be very glad, and would do all in my power to get a full house for his daughter. I would willingly also play with her on two pianos; for you would not believe how kindly her father interested himself for me in Vienna.

I do not know yet when I shall commence my journey. I shall probably be here during the hot months. The Italian Opera does not begin in Vienna till September, so I have no occasion to hurry. The Rondo for the new Concerto is not ready yet. I have not been in the right mood to finish it. When the Allegro and Adagio are quite done with, I shall not be in any anxiety about the *Finale*.

The Adagio in E major is conceived in a romantic, quiet, half melancholy spirit. It is to give the impression of the eye resting on some much loved landscape which awakens pleasant recollections, such as a lovely spring moon-light night. I have written for the violins to accompany *con sordini*. Will that have a good effect ? Time will show.

Write and tell me when you are coming back to Warsaw, for it would be worse than it was the first time if I had to give my concert without you. You do not know how I love you. Oh, if I could only prove it! What would I not give to be able to embrace you heartily once again.

Warsaw, August 21st, 1830.

This is my second letter to you. You will scarcely think it possible, but so it is.

I wrote to you directly after my prosperous return to Warsaw, but as my parents stopped at Count Skarbek's, at *Zelazowa Wola,* I, of course stopped too, and in the hurry forgot to post my letter. But there is nothing bad in the world that has not some good in it.

Perhaps I shall not weary you so much with this as with the last letter, when I had the image of your quiet country life, which I had just quitted, constantly before my eyes. I may say, truly, that I recall it with delight; I always feel a certain longing after your beautiful country seat. I do not forget the weeping willow, that Arbaleta! Oh, with what pleasure do I remember it! You have teased me enough about it to punish me for all my sins. Let me tell you what I have done since you left, and what is settled about my departure.

I was especially interested with Paër's opera, " Agnese," because Fräulein Gladkowska made her *début* in it. She looks better on the stage than in a drawing-room. Her first-rate tragic acting leaves nothing to be desired, and her vocalization, even to the high F sharp or G, is excellent. Her *nuances* are wonderful, and if her voice was rather tremulous at first, through nervousness, she sang afterwards with certainty and smoothness. The opera was curtailed which, perhaps, did not make it seem so tedious to me. The harp romance which Fräulein Gladkowska sang in the second act was very fine. I was quite enraptured. She was recalled at the conclusion of the opera, and greeted with unbounded ovations.*

In a week's time Fräulein Watkow † is to play the *rôle* of Fiorilla, in the opera of " Il Turco in Italia," which will be sure to please the public better. A great many people blame the opera of " Agnese," without knowing why.

I do not contend that Soliva ‡ might have chosen something better for Gladkowska ; " Vestalin " would, perhaps, have been more suitable, but "Agnese" is beautiful also ; the music has many

---

* Fräulein Gladkowska was the realization of Chopin's ideal His thoughts of her are interwoven into all the compositions which he wrote at that time Dreaming of her, he wrote the Adagio of the E minor Concerto ; his desire of leaving Warsaw vanished ; she entirely filled the soul of the passionate youth of twenty. Constantia Gladkowska, a pupil of Soliva, was married in 1832, and left the stage, to the great regret of all connoisseurs.

† Fräulein Wotkow, a fellow pupil with Gladkowska, also left the stage on her marriage, in 1836.

‡ Signore Soliva, an Italian by birth, went to the Warsaw Conservatoire in 1821 as singing master. When the institution was closed by the Russian Government, he migrated first to St Petersburg, then to Paris, where he died, in 1851. Soliva composed the operas, " La Testa di bronzo," " Elena e Mauvina," and several smaller works.

good points, which the young *debutante* brought out capitally.

And now what am I to do ?

I start next month, but I must first try my Concerto, for the Rondo is ready now.

Warsaw, August 31st, 1830.

It was high time for your letter to arrive, for as soon as I received it, I lost my catarrh. Would that my letters might be endowed with the same miraculous power.

I still stay here, and nothing, indeed, attracts me abroad. But I am certain to go next month, in obedience to my calling, and my reason, which must be weak, if it were not strong enough to conquer all other inclinations.

This week I must try the whole of the E minor Concerto, with quartet accompaniment, to give me confidence, as Elsner says the first orchestral trial will not go well. Last Saturday, I tried the Trio, and, perhaps, because I had not heard it for so long, was satisfied with myself. " Happy man," you will say, won't you ? It then struck me that it would be better to use the Viola instead of the Violin, as the first string predominates in the Violin, and in my Trio is hardly used at all. The viola would, I think, accord better with the 'cello. The Trio will then be ready to print. So much about myself. Now something as to the other musicians.

Last Saturday, Soliva brought forward his second pupil, Fraulein Wotkow, who delighted the whole house with her natural grace and good acting, also with her beautiful eyes and pearly teeth. She was more charming on the stage than any of our actresses. I scarcely recognized her voice at first, she was so agitated. But she acted so excellently, no one would have supposed her to be a *debutante*. Notwithstanding the encores and the enormous applause she received, she did not overcome her embarassment till the second act, when the capabilities of her voice revealed themselves, though not quite so fully as at the rehearsal, and at the performance the day before yesterday.

In vocal ability Fraulein Wotkow is far surpassed by Fraulein Gladkowska. If I had not myself heard the former I should not have believed there could be such a difference between two singers. Ernemann shares our opinion, that it is not easy to find a singer equal to Gladkowska, especially in the bell-like purity of her intonation, and true warmth of feeling, which are only properly displayed on the stage. She entrances her hearers. Wotkow made several slight mistakes, whilst with Gladkowska one did not hear a single note that was in the least doubtful, although she has only performed twice in " Agnese."

When I saw the two vocalists the day before yesterday and presented your compliments to them, they were evidently gratified and commissioned me to thank you.

Wotkow's reception was warmer than Gladkowska's, which Soliva did not seem to like.   He said
to me, yesterday, that he did not wish Wotkow
to win more applause than her fellow pupil.   I think
a considerable share of the approbation is to be
ascribed to the character which pleases the public
better (captivated also by the young girl's beauty)
than the tragic misery of the unhappy daughter in
Paer's opera.   Gladkowska is to appear shortly in
the " Diebischen Elster," but this " shortly " will
last till I am over the mountains.   Perhaps you will
then be in Warsaw, and will give me your opinion of
the performance.   Her third *rôle* is to be " Vestalin."

Warsaw, October 5th, 1830.

I was longing very much for your letter, which
has somewhat soothed me.   You cannot conceive
how impatient and wearied (a feeling I cannot
struggle against) I am of everything here.   After
the orchestral trial of my second Concerto, it was
decided that I should appear with it at the
Theatre on Monday, 11th instant.   Although this
does not quite suit me, I am curious to know
what effect the composition will have on the
public.   I hope the Rondo will produce a good
impression generally.   Soliva said, " il vous fait
beaucoup d'honneur ; " Kurpinski thought it contained originality, and Elsner an especially piquant
rhythm.   To arrange a good concert, in the true

sense of the word, and to avoid the unfortunate clarionet and flageolet solos, Mdlles. Gladkowska and Wotkow will give some solo numbers. As to overtures I will not have the one either to "Leszek," or to "Lodoiska," but that to "William Tell."

You would hardly imagine the difficulty I had to obtain permission for the ladies to sing. The Italian granted it readily, but I had to go to a higher authority still: to the Minister Mostowski, who finally agreed, for it makes no difference to him. I do not know yet what they will sing, but Soliva tells me that a chorus will be necessary for one of the arias.

I am certain not to be in Warsaw a week after the concert. My trunk is bought, the outfit ready, the score corrected, the pocket handkerchiefs hemmed, the new stockings and the new coat tried on, &c. Only the leave-taking remains, and that is the hardest of all.

Warsaw, October 12th, 1830.

MY DEAREST,

The concert, yesterday, was a perfect success; I hasten to inform you of it. I was not in the least anxious, and played as if I had been at home. The hall was crammed. Gorner's symphony opened the ball; then I played the first Allegro from the E minor Concerto; the notes seemed to roll along of themselves on the Streicher piano. A roar of applause

followed.   Soliva was very satisfied ; he conducted
his Aria, with chorus, which was very well sung by
Fräulein Wotkow.   She looked like a fairy in her
light blue dress.   After this Aria came my Adagio
and Rondo, and then the usual interval.   Connoisseurs and lovers of music came on to the stage
and complimented me on my playing, in the most
flattering manner.

The second part began with the *Tell* Overture.
Soliva conducted capitally, and the impression it
produced was deep and abiding.   The Italian was
really so good to me that I owe him my everlasting
gratitude.   He afterwards conducted the Cavatina
from " La Donna del Lago," which Fräulein Gladkowska sung.   She wore a white dress, had roses in
her hair, and looked charmingly beautiful.   She has
never sung as she did last evening, except in the air
in " Agnese."   " O, quanto lagrime per te versai,"
and the " tutto detesto " were heard splendidly, even
to the low B.   Zielinski declared that this B alone
was worth a thousand ducats.

When I had led the ladies from the stage I played
my Fantasia on National Airs.   This time I understood myself, the orchestra understood me, and the
public understood us both.   The Mazovian air, at
the end, made a great sensation.   I was so raptur-
ously applauded that I had to appear four times to
bow my thanks.   And, be assured, I did it quite
gracefully, for Brandt had fully instructed me.   If
Soliva had not taken my score home and corrected

it, and, as conductor, restrained me when I wanted to run away, I do not know what would have happened. He kept us all so splendidly in check that I never played so comfortably with an orchestra before. The Streicher piano was very much liked, but Fraulein Wotkow still more.

I am thinking of nothing but my packing up. On Saturday or Wednesday I go out into the wide world.

Ever your truly affectionate
FREDERIC.

This last concert, therefore, called forth the most favourable and enthusiastic notices of Chopin. The Warsaw newspapers were all full of his praises. They compared him to the chief European *virtuosi*, and prophesied the most brilliant future, saying that some day Poland would be justly proud of the great pianist and composer, &c., &c.

The sad but very important day in the life of a young artist, that on which he leaves his father's house, drew near. Frederic had to part, for a lengthened period, from all that was dearest to him, home, parents, sisters, and also from that lovely young *artiste*, the ideal object of his enthusiastic love. He was to leave her, and, alas! for ever.

On November 2nd, 1830, he said adieu to his beloved parents, who gave him their blessing, and embraced his sisters with tearful eyes. From

Warsaw he went first to Kalisz, where he expected
to meet his friend, Titus Woyciechowski, to travel
with him to Vienna, through Breslau and Dresden.
A circle of friends, of which the venerable Elsner
was one, accompanied Frederic to Wola (the first
village beyond Warsaw) where the pupils of the
Conservatoire awaited him and sang a cantata, composed for the occasion by Elsner. At the banquet
given there in his honour, a silver goblet, of artistic
workmanship filled to the brim with his native earth,
was presented to him. The sight of this beautiful
and ingenious gift caused the shining, art-loving eyes
of Frederic to fill with tears of the deepest emotion.

"May you, wherever you go, never forget your
fatherland, or cease to love it with a warm and
faithful heart," said the friend who presented him
the goblet in the name of them all. "Think of
Poland, think of your friends, who are proud to call
you their countryman, who expect great things from
you, whose wishes and prayers accompany you."

The young artist once more pressed the hand of
each, and then turned his steps onwards. Before
him lay the wide, checkered, unknown world; but
the consciousness of a true aim and a green blossom-
ing hope sustained him.

CHAPTER VII.

THE CLASSIC AND ROMANTIC ELEMENTS IN POLISH LITERATURE.
INFLUENCE OF THE ROMANTIC SCHOOL ON CHOPIN. HIS FIRST COMPOSITIONS.

T O the lover and especially to the *connoisseur* of music it will be interesting to make a more thorough examination of Chopin's compositions, in order to appreciate them rightly, and to learn with what intellectual equipment he set out on his long years of travel. His first works were written in a period of apparent quietness and calm. After the battle of Waterloo, which had happened during the peaceful labours of the Vienna Congress, the nations once more breathed freely ; the great conqueror was in captivity, and the political relations of the European States seemed for the time settled. Peace, so much desired, had succeeded at length to the long and sanguinary wars, and brought with it the hope of quickened life and renewed effort.

Poland, like every other country, grew conscious of its own powers, its pride revived, and patriotic reformers were energetic in diffusing plans for the amelioration of its internal affairs. By degrees chaos resolved itself into order, foreign influences were shaken off, and foreign customs discarded. Despite the miseries the country had suffered, some enthusiasts dreamed that the golden age of the Jagellons was about to return. Men of science were astir in the field of discovery, and eagerly seeking to throw fresh light on established truths. For years the garlands of fame had been won by bold warriors, and subtle politicians; now, poet, artist, and *savant* were to gather *their* laurels on the peaceful fields of science and art. A new intellectual life, full of aspiring fancy and creative impulse, universally prevailed.

At the Vienna Congress the right of being called a "kingdom" had been granted only to the smaller portion of Poland. Although exhausted by the Napoleonic wars, and earnestly engaged in healing its own wounds, the nation was anxiously desirous of restoring culture, and encouraging literature and art. There was a general feeling that on the establishment of a new social and political order, literature—as in Germany and other countries—would find its subjects in the life and manners of the people. The outbursts of feeling, the power of conception, and the universal impulse towards expression would, it was thought, lay the foundations of a national poetry, the classic forms not being considered in harmony with the character of the Polish nation.

Following the example of some industrious collectors of Polish songs and proverbs, a brisk investigation was instituted into the literary treasures of other countries. We had at that time but one representative of the new æsthetical and philosophical ideas and poetic tendencies—Casimir Brodzinski. As professor of Polish Literature at the Warsaw University, and member of the Scientific Society, he could not directly oppose the fundamental principles of his colleagues, who belonged to the classical school; but these circumstances facilitated rather than retarded the spread of his opinions, which he propagated by his lectures at the University and by essays in the journals. These opinions were based on the principles of Kant and Schiller, on the historical study of Polish literature, and on the poétical theories of the Romantic School. Casimir Brodzinski gathered around him a band of talented young men, and a contest began, which daily became more violent and bitter, between 'the Classists and Romanticists. On one side were the advocates of the old classic principles; on the other youth, with its ready enthusiasm for everything new, with such men as Bohdan Zaleski, Sewerin Goszczynski, Anton Malczewski, Stephan Witwicki, Moritz Goslowski, and later on Slowacki and Sigismund Krasinski. Mickiewicz,* the gifted author of " Grazyna " and

---

* His poems have been translated into nearly every living language, perhaps with most success into German They have a peculiar colouring, are full of poetic inspiration, and rich in thought.

" Dziady ; " and the greatest of Polish poets, supported by the historians Lelewel and Brodzinski,
placed himself at the head of the Romantic School,
and his genius soon triumphed over its opponets.

At the time when the battle between the champions
of the two schools was raging hottest, Chopin felt
the first stirrings of creative genius. Living in the
midst of a youthful circle, enthusiastic for national
poetry, which it not unjustly regarded as the basis
of all poetry, he made research for national melodies,
and sought by careful artistic treatment to enhance
their value and give them an assured place in
musical literature. In this he succeeded more completely than any other composer. No one could
reproduce with such beauty and truth the peculiar
melancholy feeling pervading all Sarmatian melodies.

The noblest enthusiasm glows in Chopin's music :
it may be called the complement, or rather the
illustration of the new national poetry. An eminent
Polish historian says of it : " A peculiar importance
belongs to Chopin's music, because in it more than
in any other our nation is represented in the noblest
light, in the possession of an independance, hitherto
unknown. Such music springs from the same
source as our national poetry."

With respect to Chopin, the same author also
quotes the following passage from Alfred de Musset's
" Confessions d'un enfant du siecle," which characterizes, with such wonderful poetic feeling and
psychological keenness, the prevailing malady of

the age : " When the war was over, the Emperor an exile, and portraits of Wellington and Blücher, with the inscription 'Salvatoribus mundi,' adorned every wall, a new generation was beholding, with gloomy thought, the ruins of the past. In the veins of these youths flowed the same warm blood which had flooded the whole world. Everyone raved about the snows of Moscow, and the sands of Egypt, every soul was full of dreams, swelling with lofty thoughts and panting with desires which were impossible, for wherever men turned their eyes all was emptiness and desolation. The more mature believed in nothing, the learned lived in an eternal contradiction, poets preached despair. An awful hopelessness raged like a pest in the civilised world." If, according to Alfred de Musset, political and literary circumstances had exercised so baneful an effect on the younger generation in France, how much more excuse was there for such a state of things in Poland, where hope had turned into scepticism, and melancholy become a chronic evil.

The sensitive and pliant Sarmatian temperament is as susceptible to hope as to despair, but the miserable political condition of the country for generations could not but foster an inclination to melancholy. The more finely strung natures, who perhaps, maintain with difficulty the necessary equilibrium for ordinary affairs, are, of course most sensitive to such influences. Considering the political circumstances of Poland, we can only wonder that misery and despair did not lead the nation to further extremes.

Among those whose productions expressed their love for their country, and profound sorrow for its shameful debasement, Chopin, for tenderness and refinement, stands pre-eminent. His handsome aristocratic appearance, and that enthusiasm of nature, which was transfused into his music, distinguished him above his compeers. The fatal events which, at the beginning of the decade of 1830, brought Poland to the verge of ruin, could not but influence the works of every native artist. Libelt, one of the chief poets of that time, sung from the very depth of his soul:

> " Die traute Heimathe bietet uns kein Gluck,
>   Erliegt dem Vaterland das Misgeschick."

How could Chopin sing a cheerful song out of a merry heart? He would have had to assume a cheerfulness he could not feel, which to his intensely natural character would have been extremely difficult. Like every great man, he was greatest when left to the inspirations of his genius. The fire and spirit of youth, indeed, glowed in his soul, and sweet melodies flowed from his pen, but through his smile the hot tear always glistened—a tribute to his country and to his brethren fallen in her defence.

The Rondo, op. 1 (dedicated to Madame Linde) composed in 1825, and afterwards arranged as a duet, although artistically written throughout, is Chopin's weakest work. His individuality was not at that time fully developed, and Hummel's influence was unmistakable. It is no disparagement of his talents to say this, for every young pianist of that period made Hummel his model, and, moreover, every genius, however independent, begins by unconsciously imitating his favourite composers and artists. As an instance of this we need only mention Beethoven.

In the following works, the " Introduction et Polonaise brillante pour piano et 'cello " (op. 3), the Sonata in C minor, (op. 4), dedicated to Elsner, and the Trio (op. 8), which, although entitled " Premier Trio," has had no successor, the leaning towards Hummel is still evident; the motives are easily comprehensible, harmonious, clear and simple in their development, but the Variations on " Don Juan " already bear the true Chopin stamp.

In 1831, just after the appearance of this piece, R. Schumann wrote a long article in the *Allgemeine Musikalische Zeitung*, under the simple heading, " An opus 2." We quote a part of it : " Eusebius had just stepped softly into the room. You are familiar with the ironical smile on the pale face by which he tries to excite attention. I was sitting at the piano with Florestan, who is, as you are aware, one of those peculiar musicians who pre-judge everything new and extraordinary. But to-day a surprise awaited him. With the words, ' Hats off, gentlemen, a genius ! ' Eusebius laid before us a piece of music of which we were not allowed to see the

I

title. I carelessly turned over the leaves. There is something fascinating in the enjoyment of music without sound. I think, too, that every composer has his own manner of writing notes; Beethoven looks different to Mozart, just as Jean Paul's words do not look like Goethe's. But now it seemed to me as if quite strange eyes, flowers' eyes, basilisks' eyes, peacocks' eyes were gazing at me. Light dawned in places; I thought I saw Mozart's 'La ci darem la mano' entwined in a hundred chords. Leoporello seemed to be looking steadily at me, and Don Juan glided past in his white mantle. 'Now play it,' said Florestan. Eusebius consented, and we sat squeezed in a window niche to listen. He played like one inspired and brought forth an innumerable host of the most life-like forms; as if the enthusiasm of the moment had raised his fingers beyond their usual possibilities. With the exception, however, of a happy smile, Florestan only expressed his approbation by saying that these Variations might have been Beethoven's or Franz Schubert's, if these composers had been pianoforte *virtuosi*. But when he turned to the title page and read, '*La ci darem la mano*, varié pour le pianoforte par Frédéric Chopin, Oeuvre 2,' we both cried in astonishment, 'a second work!' We were dumbfounded, and could only exclaim, 'Yes, but this is something clever. Chopin—I never heard the name, who can he be? An un-mistakable genius. In the Variations, in the concluding movement and in the rondo genius shines in every bar.' "

For one of the greatest musicians in Germany to write thus enthusiastically of an Opus 2, by an unknown composer, the work must have been marked by unusual originality, creative power, and technical perfection. One of the most noteworthy of the innumerable services rendered by Robert Schumann is, that in spite of the most adverse criticism, he first paved the way for Chopin's popularity in Germany, in which endeavour he was zealously aided by his wife, the world-famed pianist, Clara Wieck Schumann.

Among Chopin's works, especially distinguished for newness of form, we place the Mazurkas, op. 6 and 7. This national dance, with its monotonous, poor, and apparently common-place rhythm, rose under Chopin's magic touch to a poetic dignity, of which no Polish musician had hitherto dreamed. I have already mentioned how carefully and persever-ingly Chopin listened to and assimilated the national songs; he eliminated all vulgarity from the rhythm, and retained only its characteristic element, while the melody he idealised and glorified with his finest poetry. Thus arose that exquisite series of mazurkas, filled with gladness and melancholy, smiles and tears. The two works referred to form, so to speak, the first links in the chain.

In a foreign country, hundreds of miles from his beloved home, Chopin often felt an indescribable yearning for his family and fatherland. At such times art was his only, and indeed his best solace. His piano was his confidant, and for hours he would pour out his feelings in sweet melancholy strains : the tones-poems thus composed being among the finest which ever flowed from his pen. This mazurka form, peculiar to the Poles, seemed to reveal a particular phase of feeling shared in more or less by all Chopin's contemporaries. The mazurka is the musical expression of a national yearning, and is to every Slav singularly full of charm and sympathy.

The three Nocturnes (op. 9) are true Petrarchian sonnets, overflowing with grace, fairy-like charm, and captivating sweetness ; they seem like whisperings, on a still summer night, under the balcony of the beloved one. Chopin writes : "I have the *cognoscenti* and the poetic natures on my side." But the reviewers appear to have belonged to neither category, for the reception they gave to the nocturnes was to put their heads together and say, "he has stolen it from Field !" They even went so far as to assert that Chopin was a pupil * of that composer, who was then living in St. Petersburg. †

---

* See Schilling's Universal Lexicon of Music.

† John Field, born in Dublin, in 1782, a pupil of Clementi, was one of the greatest and most celebrated pianists of his time. In 1804, he went to St. Petersburg, where, except for some artistic tours, he resided till 1820. He died in Moscow in 1837.

There exists, at all times, a species of half-educated, envious criticism, ever ready to support mediocre talent, and to stifle the first germs of genius. Chopin felt its sting. Foremost among such opponents was Rellstab, of Berlin, who, in his journal, the *Iris*, wrote disparagingly of Chopin's talents and compositions. Sikorski, on the other hand, well-known as one of the best and most conscientious of Polish critics, says : "On comparing Field's nocturnes with those of Chopin, it must be candidly confessed that the former do not surpass the latter; although it is not to be denied that in spite of some striking Chopin traits, opus 9 somewhat resembles Field's works in depth of feeling and particular turns of expression. Their differences may be thus described : Field's nocturnes represent a cheerful, blooming landscape, bathed in sunshine ; while Chopin's depict a romantic, mountainous region, with a dark back-ground, and lowering clouds flashing forth lightning."

Worthy of mention among Chopin's early works are the "Variations brillantes" (op. 12), "Grandes Etudes" (op. 10), and some very interesting pieces with orchestral accompaniments, written between 1828—30, for example, "Grand Fantaisie sur des airs polonais" (op. 13), "Cracovienne" (op. 14), and two Concertos, of which the one in E minor was composed before his last journey from Warsaw. The Fantasia and Rondo are almost unknown to the German public, although distinguished by an originality never wanting in Chopin's works. The technical difficulties, and the specifically Polish character of the earlier works have, perhaps, hindered their popularity. But this is not the case with the Concertos in E minor (op. 11), and F minor (op. 21.)* Chopin's spiritual kinsman, Robert Schumann, valued them very highly, and made merry over their opponents, whom he jocosely likened to the French, in the time of Louis Philippe, refusing to recognize the legitimate Duke of Modena as King, because he had ascended the throne by a revolution.

Chopin never imitated other composers; and never suffered himself to be misled by unjust blame or vulgar praise. The approval of genuine musicians gave him pleasure, but we can say of him, as we cannot of everyone, that he never courted distinctions or applause. This noble feature of his character was sometimes inimical to his interests, for the gentlemen of the press are not best pleased when a poet and artist pays no homage to their power by asking for their help and favour.

In 1834, Schumann wrote, in his "Gesammelte Schriften über Musik und Musiker," vol. 1, p. 275: " We may incidentally refer to a famous jackass of a

---

* I will not refer to the other works produced between 1824-9, and first published after Chopin's death by Julius Fontana, as the composer did not himself desire their publication.

newspaper which, as we hear, (for we do not read it, and flatter ourselves that in this we are not quite unlike Beethoven) sometimes glances at us, under its mask, with its dagger-like eyes, and only because we jokingly suggested that the member of their staff who wrote about Chopin's Don Juan Variations resembled a bad verse, with a couple of feet too much, which it was proposed to lop off at leisure. But why should I recall this to-day, when I have just come from Chopin's F minor Concerto? Beware! Milk, cool blue milk *versus* poison. For what is a whole year of newspapers to a Chopin concerto? What is master of arts madness to poetic madness? What are ten editorial crowns to an *adagio* in the second concerto? . . . Chopin does not present himself with an orchestral army like the great geniuses, he has only a little cohort, but this is devoted to him to the last man."

Chopin's friend and brother artist, Franz Liszt, the greatest pianist of the present century, although not sharing Schumann's unbounded enthusiasm, always pays due recognition to Chopin's talents, and occasionally the tribute of his supreme admiration. Speaking of the two Concertos, Chopin would, he thinks, have preferred greater freedom, but did violence to the promptings of his genius in order to conform to the old-fashioned rules of composition. Liszt says: " These works are distinguished by a style of rare excellence, and contain passages of great interest, phrases of astonishing grandeur. Take, for example, the *Adagio* in the second Concerto, for which he had a decided preference himself, and was in the habit of frequently performing. The accessory figures display the composer's happiest manner, while the proportions of the chief phrase of the fundamental subject are wonderfully grand. This subject, with a recitative in the minor, forms the antistrophe. The whole movement is ideally perfect, now radiant with joy, now melting in pity."

I feel bound, in conclusion, to supplement the criticisms of Schumann and Liszt, at that time the only representatives of the so-called music of the future, by an opinion formed at the present day, and unbiased, therefore, by the prejudices and controversies to which our master's creative genius gave rise. The younger generation of musicians—and the pianists in particular—having, in a great measure, studied Chopin from their early youth, know how to appreciate him, for we can only truly estimate what we are thoroughly acquainted with, and which has, so to speak, become to us a second nature. The discussion as to Chopin's *status* in the musical world is over, and his high position assigned to him once for all. It is, however, interesting to read the criticism of one of the most gifted pianists of the present day, Hermann Scholtz. In a letter, which I here quote, he says, speaking of Chopin's earliest compositions :

" In considering these works, we are most astonished at the great productiveness which he displayed in early

youth. What a wealth of melody, harmony, and rhythm
appears even in these first compositions! His originality
is marvellous, for at a period when other composers are
more or less dependant on models, with him everything
is new. He is rightly called the creator of a new pianoforte music; for who before him wrote for the instrument
as he did? in whom do we find such nobility of thought,
such spiritualization of passages? I will merely remind
you of the manner in which he treated the left hand.
His tone-poems in the dance form (especially his
mazurkas and polonaises) receive an unusual charm
from their national colouring.

"Among his weakest compositions are the 'Rondo,
op, 1,' 'Sonata, op. 4,' and 'Rondo à la Mazur, op. 5,'
which in form leaves much to be desired, but, by its
melodic charm and grace of feeling, is so irresistably
fascinating that its weaknesses are more than counter-
balanced. Exception might be taken to the instru-
mentation of the 'Cracovienne,' the Fantasia on Polish
airs, the Variations on 'Don Juan,' and the two Concertos, but on examining the pianoforte part we find it
full of the most beautiful thoughts, besides an unusual
number of passages quite new of their kind and afford-
ing ample opportunity for the display of the pianist's
virtuosity. I would particularly mention the *Larghetto*,
from the second Concerto, a piece full of poetic charm.
In it all the attributes of a perfect work of art appear in
the happiest union: noble melody, choice harmonies,
agreeable figures, and the perfection of form, while the
thoroughly original ideas are finely contrasted. One
thing, indeed, is frequently lacking in Chopin's

compositions—especially in those written in the larger forms—the thematic work, which is the *point d'appui* in the works of Beethoven and the older masters. In view of his undeniable excellencies, we readily look with indulgence on these minor failings in an artist of such rare imaginative power as Chopin, who, while revealing to his hearers a new world of thought, is himself, completely absorbed in the creations of his fancy, for which reason most of his shorter works give the impression of an improvisation.

" Chopin gives us his finest and most finished work in the smallest forms, such as the nocturnes, in which we see the real enthusiasm of his nature; his studies even are redolent with poetry. Play numbers 3, 6, 9, 10, and 12 from op. 10, and you cannot fail to agree with me. I consider the last study (in C minor), with its heroic character, as the most beautiful in this collection. To Chopin is due the merit of having first used the broken chords in a spread-out form, which had formerly been written only in a close position. To this innovation we owe a host of interesting figures, as his studies and concertos abundantly prove. The transposition of the third and other intervals to a higher octave produces that agreeable effect which is so captivating in his music. Chopin may possibly have received a suggestion from Weber, who used plenty of firm chords in a scattered position.

" One of Chopin's special characteristics is the employment of the diminished chord, especially the chord of the seventh. This frequently occurs in his mazurkas, in which, by the enharmonic use of this chord, he accomplishes a charming return to the chief subject. We must point out a passage in the Etude in A flat, No. 10, op. 10, in which, by an enharmonic change of the ordinary chord of the seventh, the chief melody re-enters on the chord of the six-four, which produces an effect quite bewitching. We meet with similar examples in Schumann's Romance (F sharp) and Mendelssohn's 'Songs without Words' (No. 1, book 2.) Wagner, also, has turned this modulation to the happiest account in his newest operas.

"Another of Chopin's pecularities is that he always repeats the chief thought in a new form, and by arabesques or fresh harmonization always gives it an additional interest."

With such an intellectual equipment, of whose greatness he was not himself conscious, Chopin went abroad. Granting that his creative talent developed in after years, and that he daily gained fresh stores of knowledge and experience, we still maintain that, as regards real inspiration, he was never grander or more independent than in his first works. They glow with that inimitable youthful fire, which no one possesses for more than a limited period, but which produces an unfailing delight and an indelible impression.

CHAPTER VIII.

*GERMAN AND ITALIAN MUSIC IN THE YEARS
1827—1831. JOHANN MATUSZYNSKI.*

THE goal of Chopin's travels was Italy, the land
still glorious in fame, the land of love, the
cradle of the arts. In the home of the great masters,
where sweet melodies are heard in every mouth, he
hoped to perfect himself in the practice of his art,
and to gather fresh thoughts for new works.

In Germany, music had, by the first quarter of the
present century, attained a high position; such men
as Handel, Glück, Haydn, Mozart, Beethoven, and
Weber had enriched the world with masterpieces;
all the larger towns possessed a good opera house,
and the best singers and instrumentalists were heard
in the concert halls. But the *repertoires* consisted
almost exclusively of Italian music, especially of the
works of that most prolific writer and universal
favourite, Gioacchino Rossini. Mozart's operas
were rarely heard: "Der Freischütz" was the only
German opera that had attained any popularity;
"Fidelio" met with so little success that, after one

performance in Vienna, it was withdrawn, and, as was then thought, finally.

Beethoven's immortal works, however highly *connoisseurs* might esteem them, were lying unheeded in libraries. The *chefs d'orchestres*, either from indolence, personal grudge, or because they were envious of the master who had surpassed all other composers, showed little readiness to study his wonderful creations ; besides which, the players of that time were seldom technically qualified for the difficult task of adequately rendering Beethoven's Symphonies. The more easily comprehensible music of the Italian school was received by the public with great *gusto*, and only a few isolated voices were heard asking for deeper and more earnest works.

Although Beethoven had been sleeping three years in the Wahringer churchyard, at Vienna, nothing of his music was heard beyond an occasional performance of his larger works at the Vienna " Spiritual oder Gesellschafts-Concerten," or the production of one of the last quartets by Schuppanzigh, who received but little thanks for his pains.* Beethoven's Sonatas had as completely vanished from the piano as if they had been buried with their author. By a considerable section of the public his glorious

---

* From 1827 to 1832 there was only *one* performance of a Beethoven Symphony at the " Spirituel " concerts. The one given was the C minor. (See Hanslick's " Geschichte des Concertwesens in Wien."

Pianoforte Concertos, and the Violin Concerto were thought wearisome, and almost unplayable ; only by a very small and select minority was the master sincerely reverenced and warmly admired. Through their exertions to make his works accessible to the general public, his fame gradually increased, till, like the sun long struggling through its clouds, it shone over the whole civilised world.

How often must the master have been cut to the heart at seeing how small was the number of those who understood him, and how many of his country-men exclusively preferred Italian music. But every lofty genius is aware of the real measure of its own greatness : mediocre ability over-estimates itself, great talent knows what are its capacities, but genius despite much or long misunderstanding, and uninfluenced by praise or blame, goes on its way, trusting to the voice within which ever and again cries, " your time is coming."

Beethoven made no secret of his opinions, and, regardless of giving offence, spoke out plainly against the French and Italian music of his day. To this Schindler, in his Biography of Beethoven, refers as follows : " At the beginning of the third decade of the present century, when the flood of Italian music was at its height, Beethoven was one day conversing with some friends on the almost desperate prospects of musical art, when we heard him say decisively, ' But they cannot deprive me of my place in the history of art.' " This clearly shows that sure confidence about the future consoled him for the lack of present success.

Under such circumstances the generality of compositions were, of course, of an insipid kind, designed only for external effect. The famous pianists of the day—Field, Cramer, Klengel (pupils of Clementi), and Hummel (pupil of Dionys Weber) *—gradually disappeared from the scene of the triumphs of Field as a *virtuoso,* and of Hummel as a composer and tasteful player. Among a younger generation of musicians, Kalkbrenner bore the palm; after him came Moscheles, Herz, Thalberg, and Mendelsohn. Liszt had not made a name till some years later. Felix Mendelssohn had attracted attention by his instrumental works, but his fame was then merely in the bud. Franz Schubert † was only known in Vienna and Prague as a song-writer. In Vienna, where he was born and lived for the whole of his short life, people knew nothing, or cared nothing, about his C major Symphony.

A little band of true lovers of art, men to whom music was something sacred, strove to bring about a reform, and shrunk not from material sacrifices in

---

* Dionys Weber, born 1771, died 1842, founded the Prague Conservatoire in 1811. He was a good composer and an excellent teacher. Under his management the Prague Conservatoire became one of the best in Europe.

* Born January 31st, 1797, died November 18th, 1828. His grave is close to Beethoven's.

the cause of earnest music. Deeming the encouragement of young and struggling artists a *desideratum*
they offered prizes for the best symphony, which
were competed for from time to time, as, in 1834,
when Lachner won the first prize. Attracted by
the honour and pecuniary advantages there was
no lack of competitors, but although most of the
compositions displayed knowledge, industry, and
conscientious work, none of them were illumined by
the immortal spark of genius.   It was at length perceived that no amount of prize-giving would produce
genius, or even talent; that the true musician, like
the poet, must be *born;* and the scheme was
abandoned.

The German masters of that day were more
successful in the domain of opera than in that of
symphony; Winter's " Das unterbrochene Opfer-
fest," Weigl's " Schweizerfamilie," Spohr's " Jes-
sonda," " Azor und Zemire," and " Faust," were
favourably received for upwards of twenty years.
Of Kreutzer's works, " Das Nachtlager von Granada "
has alone been preserved, of Marschner's (the greatest
opera composer of the three we have mentioned)
" Der Templar und die Judin " and " Hans Heiling "
have remained on the stage.   Lortzing, a writer of
comic operas, came out later, as also did Flotow.
Meyerbeer, whose " Robert le Diable," and " Les
Huguenots " have now been over the whole world,
had then, with the exception of his " Ritter des
Kreuzes," only written operas for the Italian stage,

but had been unable to compete with the highly-admired Rossini.

Italy could no longer boast illustrious *virtuosi* like Corelli, Tartini, Viotti, Scarlatti, and Clementi, whose genius had attracted the eyes of all Europe; but she possessed a Paganini, the greatest violinist of the century, as Catalini was the greatest singer. Spohr, in his autobiography, says a great deal in disparagement of Paganini, not, indeed, from jealousy, for, being himself one of the greatest violinists musical, history can produce, he adhered as closely to the principles of the Classic School as Paganini did to those of the Romantic. Those who heard them both say, that although they could not but admire Spohr, he never carried them away with the same force, or produced such a deep undying impression as Paganini.

In 1829, Paganini appeared at several concerts in Warsaw, and Chopin was entranced by his playing. He never ceased to speak with enthusiasm of the Paganini evenings, which seemed to carry him out of the real world into a land of happy dreams.

Lipinski,* who had made Paganini's acquaintance

---

* Charles Lipinski, born at Rdzyn, in Poland, in 1790, was as great a violonist as Chopin was a pianist. He enjoyed a considerable reputation; but as a composer is so far surpassed by Chopin that the two can only be mentioned together as Poland's greatest *virtuosi* Lipinski died in 1861, at his estate in Galicia, after holding, for more than twenty years, the post of chef d'orchestre at Dresden.

K

at Piacenza, met him again in Warsaw, and the two artists greeted each other with the sincerest pleasure. In spite of all the honour paid to the great Italian, it was felt that Polish patriotism was in question, and this showed itself very warmly. A competition was proposed, which the two artists accepted; they each played their favourite pieces in turn, and concluded with a double Concerto by Kreutzer,* amid frantic shouts of applause.

The modesty of Chopin's character and his freedom from jealousy appear from a remark which he made on this occasion, " If I were such a pianist as Paganini is a violinist I should like to engage in a similar competition with a pianist of equal powers." That evening he made up his mind to pay a long visit to Paganini's fatherland ; no less did the singers attract him " to the land where the citrons bloom," for Italy had at that day a more brilliant array of vocal artists than any country in Europe. The mild climate of those happy regions is favourable to the development of fine voices ; but the Italian singing masters understand also the art of bringing out the voice to the best advantage.

The Italian composers, Rossini, Mercadente, Vaccai, Bellini, and Donizetti wrote excellently

---

* Rudolph Kreutzer, not to be confounded with Conradin Kreutzer, was born in 1766, at Versailles, of German parents. He was a great *virtuoso*, wrote several brilliant Concertos, and some incomparable studies. He died in 1831, at Geneva.

for the voice, but they not only required a fine, rich organ, but an artistic culture, such as in these days, unfortunately, is rare. What a stimulus to fresh effort Chopin hoped to receive from hearing Rubini, Mario, Galli, Lablache, Tamburin, Pasta, Judith, Grusi, and Palazzesi!

In Poland, Italian opera was considered the finest in the world. Every great city, like London, Paris, Vienna, St. Petersburg, or Stockholm, had an Italian opera house; even in such cities as Dresden and Munich there was an Italian as well as a German opera, or at least Italian singers were engaged besides German ones.

Had Chopin gone to Italy his playing would undoubtedly have captivated a people so sensitive to artistic beauty, and it is possible that the voice of praise might have rendered him insensible to other influences; but as a mere listener he had been learning to admire, and criticise the achievements of others.

Mozart, to whom Chopin looked up with reverence, had visited Italy when fourteen years of age, and won great triumphs as a pianist, but as soon as he had heard the glorious voices and perfect vocalization of the operatic singers, he felt stirred by the desire of writing an opera. In 1770, he composed " Midritate Rè di Ponta," and the success of this work made him resolve to devote his energies thenceforth more especially to the stage. In no other country could a composer attain such operatic triumphs; the report of a new and well-received opera ran like wild-fire from town to town, and the fame of a young composer spread from the Italian cities over the whole world.

Meyerbeer also began his career as a pianist, and as such achieved a brilliant success. Salieri, hearing him improvise at Vienna, at once discerned his ability, and said to him, "What are you going to do? Go to Italy, and study the operatic style, and the Italian method of singing." Through the influence of his wealthy family, Meyerbeer's first operatic attempts had been produced at the Royal Theatre in Berlin, but had excited little interest. To the somewhat dispirited young writer, Salieri's advice seemed very acceptable. He acted upon it, and when he had been some months in Milan, wrote an operetta, which had a very favourable reception. After an interval of a year he produced the "Crociato in Egitto," which carried the name of Meyerbeer all over Italy. Although not quite twenty years of age, the doors of the Royal Academy of Music in Paris were opened to him, and they were the key to those of the entire musical world.

Many of Chopin's friends and admirers used to say, "Our Frederic will do likewise, and become a first rate operatic composer." For him, however, a different though a still splendid destiny was in store. The non-fulfilment of these expectations, to which his rare musical gifts had given rise, may be explained by external circumstances.

It seems at first sight a matter of surprise that Chopin did not produce one dramatic work during his many years' residence in Paris, where there is such an abundance of good models and first-rate artists ; besides which there was at that time not only the Grand Opera, but the Comic and Italian operas.   But no one fully acquainted with the circumstances will be astonished that, in Paris, Chopin should have held aloof from the stage.   In Italy, a new opera can be mounted without much expense, for the public care little about costumes and scenery.   They attend the opera solely for the music : if this finds favour and the singers are good a new work may be performed, several nights in succession, and the fortune of the composer is made. But in Paris a new opera necessitates a large outlay, besides which—and particularly in the case of a foreigner—a famous reputation and influential patronage are requisite for the acceptance of any great operatic work.   The Parisians demand a mounting at once tasteful and gorgeous, and every opera— whatever the excellence of the music—must include some brilliant dances in order to produce a due effect.   Otherwise a *fiasco* may be predicted with something like certainty.

When Chopin settled in Paris he had to take thought for means of subsistence, in order to render needless any further pecuniary sacrifices on the part of his parents.   In spite of his masterly skill he did not find it easy to gain a footing in a city, where

there were already many pianists of talent and
celebrity.   In the winter famous performers from
all parts of Europe resorted to the capital of the
continent to let their light shine before the leaders of
fashion. To keep abreast of such competitors Chopin
was compelled to study continuously, and only a
virtuoso knows what this means.   Neither could he
abandon society, although this would have been
better for his delicate health.   If he could have
lived according to his inclinations as a composer,
not as an executant, and a Scribe had written a
libretto for him, an opera might then have been
included among his productions in Paris.

But we have been anticipating and must return
to our artist, whose beautiful, dreamy eyes beamed
with delight as he thought of Italy, the ideal land of
his imagination. He was subject, of course, to seasons
of depression, and yearning after his beloved family,
for his was not one of those superficial natures which
soon forgets what is not before its eyes. He thought
fondly of parents and sisters, and of his adored
Constantia with all the passionate ardour of his
poetic soul. Her sweet voice was ever ringing in his
ears, and in his dreams he saw her eyes suffused
with tears ; while the ring which she had slipped on
his finger at parting was his dearest jewel.   His
letters to his confidential friend, Johann Matuszynski,
show how noble and fervent was his love, yet
Constantia's name never once appears in his
letters to his family, from whom he kept secret his

attachment. He used earnestly to beg his friend to send him frequent news of his " angel of peace," as he called his Constantia, that he might not perish with longing and unrest.

As this friend faithfully fulfilled what was required of him, a brief reference may be made to his life. Johann Matuszynski was born in Warsaw, December 9th, 1809, and, after passing through the Lyceum, went to the University to study medicine. At the end of six terms of diligent study, he was appointed regimental surgeon in 1830, just when the war of freedom broke out in Poland. Four years later he graduated at Tübingen, and received the diploma of doctor of medicine and surgery. At the same time he wrote a treatise on " Plica Polonica," which was highly commended. He next went to Paris, where he immediately visited his friend Chopin, whom he had not seen for five years. They had been school-fellows at the Lyceum, and as the doctor was an excellent flautist they had as boys played duets together. A weakness of the chest obliged Matu-szynski, in after years, to abandon his instrument.

In Paris he soon attracted the attention of the first physicians, and, what for a foreigner is very rare, was made professor at the "Ecole de Médicine." Proud of this position, he devoted himself to his profession with an assiduity injurious to his delicate health, and he died of consumption, April 20th, 1842.

CHAPTER IX.

CHOPIN'S STAY IN BRESLAU, DRESDEN, PRAGUE, AND VIENNA.

AT Kaliz, where Frederic met his friend and travelling companion, Titus Woyciechowski, he was the guest of the physician, Dr. Kelbich. That most agreeable man requested him to give a concert in the little town, but the young artist declined, not being satisfied with the orchestra.

At the present day, a famous pianoforte *virtuoso* like Chopin would not concern himself about the orchestra, but unhesitatingly perform the longest programme, without the assistance of any other artists. Then, however, pianists rarely played less than two pieces with orchestral accompaniment; they engaged the co-operation of other musicians, partly from a respect for art, partly for the sake of offering the public more variety.

Chopin declared that it was impossible to play the whole evening, and as soon as Woyciechowski arrived, he bade a grateful farewell to his hospitable host and pursued his journey. The friends stopped at Breslau, from whence Chopin wrote as follows :—

Breslau, November, 9th, 1830.

MY BELOVED PARENTS AND SISTERS,

We arrived here very comfortably on Saturday evening, at six, in bright pleasant autumn weather. We put up at the Hotel " *Zur Goldenen Gans,*" and, as soon as we had dressed and taken some refreshment, we went to the theatre, where Raimund's " Alpine King" was being performed. You will see the piece some day. The public admired the scenery more than we did. I thought the acting pretty good. The day before yesterday " Maurer and Schlosser " was given, but not in first-rate style. To-day I shall hear the " Interrupted Sacrifice ; " I am quite curious to see how it will turn out. There is a want of good singers here, but then the theatre is very cheap; a place in the pit only costs two Polish gulden.*

Breslau pleases me much better this time than last. I have delivered Sowinski's letter, but have scarcely seen him yet, for we were unfortunately out when he called. We had first gone to the *Ressource,* where, by invitation of the conductor, Schnabel, I was present at the rehearsal for the concert in the evening. There are three concerts a week.

As is often the case at rehearsals, there was a very poor orchestra; a certain Referendar Hellwig was going to perform Moscheles' E flat major Concerto.

---

* An Imperial Mark.

Before this gentleman sat down, Schnabel, who had not heard me for four years, asked me to try the piano. I could not refuse this request, and played some Variations. Schnabel overwhelmed me with expressions of praise and pleasure. This made Hellwig feel a little uneasy, and I was pressed to take his place in the evening. Schnabel threw his influence into the scale, and asked me so heartily, that I could not deny the dear old man his wish. He is a great friend of Herr Elsner's, which means much to me ; but I told Schnabel at once that I only played for his sake, that for weeks I had not touched an instrument, and that it was not part of my programme to play in Breslau. Schnabel replied, that he was well aware of that, but that when he saw me in church, yesterday, he wished to ask me, but did not venture to do so. What could I do ? So I went back to the hotel with his son to fetch my music, and played the Romance and Rondo from the second Concerto.

The Germans admired my playing at the rehearsal. " What a light touch he has," I heard them whisper ; but about the composition I did not catch a syllable. Titus, whose ears are everywhere, and who is always active on my behalf, heard one gentleman say, " there is no doubt that this young man can play, but he cannot compose."

Yesterday, at the *table d'hôte*, I made the acquaintance of a very amiable-looking gentleman, who was sitting opposite me. In the course of conversation

I discovered that his name was Scharff, that he knew Scholtz, of Warsaw, well, and was on friendly terms with the gentlemen to whom I had letters of introduction. This Herr Scharff was wonderfully kind and obliging to Titus and myself. He took us all over Breslau, went with us to the suburbs of the town, wrote down our names as guests at the *Ressource,* and procured us visitors' tickets for the concert yesterday, which he sent before the rehearsal. How astonished this friendly gentleman, and his companion who had obtained the tickets, must have been, when they beheld in one of the strangers the chief personage in the performance.

Besides playing the Rondo, I improvised, for the sake of the connoisseurs, on a theme from the "Mutes of Portice." There was an overture, and some dancing to conclude with. Schnabel wanted to regale me with a sumptuous supper, but I only took a cup of broth.

Of course I have made the acquaintance of the chief organist in Breslau, Herr Kohler; he promised to show me his organ. I met, also, a certain Baron Nesse di Neisse, a great violin player and a pupil of Spohr's.

Another musician resident here, a Herr Hesse,*

---

* Adolf Friedrich Hesse, born in Breslau 1809, died there 1863, was one of the most distinguished of organists and organ composers. He was a pupil of Kohler, whom he afterwards succeeded. By long artistic tours he acquired a brilliant reputation. In 1844 he was invited to Paris for the opening of the great organ in the church of St. Eustache.

was also very complimentary to me; but none of the Germans, except Schnabel, whose face beams with real delight, and who claps me on the shoulder every moment, quite know what to make of me.

Titus took delight in watching what went on around. As I have not yet got a name, people could not make up their minds whether to praise or to blame me, and connoisseurs were not quite certain whether my music was really good, or only seemed so. A gentleman came up to me and praised the form, as something quite new. I don't know his name, but I think of all my listeners he understood me the best.

Schnabel placed a carriage at my disposal in the kindest manner; but when the dancing began, about ten, we went quietly home. I am truly glad that I was able to give pleasure to the dear old man.

After the concert, Schnabel introduced me to a lady who is considered the first pianist in Breslau. She thanked me very much for the " delightful surprise," as she expressed it, but regretted, exceedingly, that I would not make up my mind to appear in public.

The Referendar consoled himself, and sang— though very indifferently—Figaro's air from the " Barbiere di Sevilla."

A great deal was said about Elsner, yesterday, and his Echo Variations for the orchestra were much praised. I said that they could only judge what a composer Elsner was after hearing his Coronation

Mass. We leave for Dresden to-morrow at two o'clock. I kiss and embrace you. My kindest remembrances to Messrs. Elsner, Zywny, Matuszynski, Kolberg, Marylski, and Witwicki.

Your FREDERIC.

Dresden, November 14th, 1830.

I have scarcely found a moment yet to write you a few words. I have just come from a dinner at which the company were all Poles. I have crept away to write to you, for the post goes at seven, and I should much like to see the "Mutes of Portici," at the Theatre.

We quitted Breslau unwillingly; the society of the gentlemen to whom Scholtz had given us letters of introduction made our sojourn in the capital of Silesia very agreeable.

My first visit in Dresden was to Fräulein Pechwell. She played, on Friday, at a Musical *Soirée* at Councillor Kressig's, and procured an *entrée* for me. The "Mutes" was to be performed the same evening at the theatre. The choice was difficult; but one must always be polite to ladies, so I decided for the *Soirée*. Another important reason with me was, that Signora Palazzesi,* the *prima donna* of the Italian opera, was expected to be there.

---

* Mathilde Palazzesi, an excellent Italian singer, was engaged by Morlacchi, at Dresden, in 1828, where she remained till the closing of the Italian Opera, in 1832.

After making a very careful toilet, I had a Sedan chair fetched, got into the queer, comfortable box, and was carried to the house where the musical entertainment was to take place. The spirit of mischief seized me, and I felt a desire to stamp through the bottom of the chair; however, I forebore.

Arrived at Kressig's abode, I sent up my name to Fräulein Pechwell, whereupon the master of the house appeared, received me with many compliments, and led me into a room where a number of ladies were sitting at eight large tables. No flashing of diamonds met my gaze, but the more modest glitter of a host of steel knitting needles, which moved ceaselessly in the hands of these industrious ladies.

The number of ladies and of needles was so large that if the ladies had purposed an attack upon the gentlemen, the latter would have been in a sorry plight. The only resource left them would have been to have made weapons of their spectacles, of which there were as many as there were bald heads.

The clatter of knitting needles and tea cups was suddenly interrupted by music from the adjoining room. The overture to "Fra Diavolo" was played first; then Signora Palazzesi sang, in a magnificent voice, clear as a bell, and with plenty of bravura. I presented myself to the songstress, which gave me an opportunity of speaking also to the Musical

Director, Rastrelli,* who had accompanied her.
With true artistic politeness Rastrelli introduced
me to Signor Rubini, who, with much affability,
promised me a letter to his brother, the famous
tenor.   I do not need anything more for Milan.
Yesterday, Rubini kindly took me to the Catholic
Church, where a mass was being performed of
Morlacchi's (band-master here.)   This refined and
agreeable man remembered me at once, and, giving
me a place beside him, talked to me a long time.
At these Vespers I heard the two celebrated Nea-
politan soprani, Sassaroli and Tarquinio; the violin
obligato was played by the bandmaster, the incomparable Rolla, to whom Soliva had given me a
recommendation.   Rolla received me very pleasantly,
and said he would give me a letter to his father, the
opera director in Milan.

After hearing Fraulein Pechwell play at the
musical *soirée*, I quietly slipped away to the opera;
but only arrived at the commencement of the fifth
act, so refrain from any criticism.   I shall hear it all
this evening.

As I was going at the Dresden visiting hour, to
call on Klengel, I met him in front of his house.
He knew me directly, and welcomed me with

---

* Joseph Rastrelli was musical director of the Royal Opera
in Dresden from 1823 to 1842.   He was an excellent conductor, and a good composer.   His operas, "Salvator Rosa,"
and "Bertha of Bretagne," both achieved success.

heart-felt politeness. I have a great respect for him. Klengel asked me where I lived, and begged me to come and see him early the next day, as he could not go back with me then. He advised me to play in public, but I told him, in as friendly a way as I could, that I should not be here long enough for that. I don't think Dresden would bring me either much fame, or much money, and I have no time to spare.

General Kniaziewicz, whom I saw at Frau Pruszak's, talked about a concert, but thought with me that I should make little by it.

Yesterday I heard "Tancred," but could not, on the whole, praise the performance. Rolla's marvellous solo, and the song by Fräulein von Hähnel, of the Vienna Royal Opera Theatre, had to make up for the shortcomings of the rest. The King, with his court, were present; they were, the same morning, at the service in the church, where a mass, by Baron Miltitz, was performed, under the direction of Morlacchi. The voices of Messrs. Sassarole, Muschetti, Babnigg, and Zezi sounded magnificent. I cannot call the composition original, but well worked out; the royal chamber musicians, Dotzaceer and Rummer, celebrated violincellists, played their solos very finely.

I know none of the chief artists intimately, except dear Klengel, to whom I am sure to play to-morrow. I like to talk to Klengel, for one always learns something from him.

I saw the Green Arch when I was here before,
and once is enough for me ; but I have visited the
Picture Gallery again with the greatest interest ; if
I lived here I should go every week ; there are
pictures in it, the sight of which makes me fancy
I hear music.   Good bye for to-day.

Your FREDERIC.

Prague, November 21st, 1830.

The week at Dresden slipped away so quickly that
I hardly noticed how it went.   I used to leave my
hotel in the best of spirits in the morning, and did
not return till night.   When Klengel came to know
me better as a musician, that is, when I had played
my Concerto to him, he said that my playing
strongly reminded him of Field, that my touch was
quite unique, and that, although he had already
heard much about me, he had not thought that I
was such a *virtuoso*.

I saw—and why should I be ashamed of it ?—with
pleasure, that these were sincere compliments ; and
he gave me a practical proof of their being so, for
scarcely had I left him when he went to Malacchi,
and to Councillor von Lüttichau, who is director
general of the Royal drama, to find out whether, if I
stayed four days longer in Dresden, I could give a
concert without any very burdensome preparations.
Klengel assured me afterwards that he did not do

this for me, but for Dresden, and that he should like
to force me into giving a concert. He came to me
the next morning and said, that he had taken all the
necessary steps, but that there was no evening dis-
engaged till next Sunday (this was Wednesday.)
The first performance of "Fra Diavolo" was fixed
for Friday, and Rossini's "La Donna del Lago," in
Italian, for Saturday.

I gave Klengel a hearty welcome, for, indeed, I
feel as if I had known him for years, and he seems
to feel the same towards me ; he asked for the score
of my Concerto, and took me with him to the *soirée*
at Frau Niesiolowska's. I also called on Frau
Szczerbinin, but I had stayed so long at Frau
Niesiolowska's that by the time I arrived the company had gone. I was, therefore, asked to dinner
the next day. In the afternoon I went, by invitation, to see Countess Dobrzycka, who is head
governess to Princess Augusta.

The countess was celebrating her birthday, and I
had scarcely offered my congratulations, when two
Saxon Princesses entered : Princess Augusta, only
daughter of the late King Frederic Augustus, sur-
named "the Just," and Princess Maximilian, *neé*
Princess of Lucca, daughter-in-law of the present
King, a pleasant young lady.

I played before these ladies, whereupon letters
were promised me for Italy, which showed that my
playing must have pleased them. Two letters were
in fact sent to my hotel the next day ; the Countess

Dobrzycka will send the others after me to Vienna. I gave her my address there. The letters were addressed to the Queen of the Sicilies, at Naples, and Princess Ellasino, at Rome. Letters of recommendation were also promised me to the reigning Duchess of Lucca, and the Viceroy of Milan, which I was to receive through the kin⁴ care of Kraszewski.

Klengel has just given me a letter to Vienna, where he thinks of going himself bye and bye. At Frau Niesiolowska's he drank my health in champagne. The lady of the house teased me a good deal, and insisted on always calling me " Szopski."

Rolla is a first-rate violinist, as anyone who knows anything about violin playing must admit.

Goodbye till you hear from Vienna, which we hope to reach by nine on Thursday morning.

I pleased General Kniaziewicz very much ; he told me that no other pianist had made such an agreeable impression on him ; I tell you this because I know you will like to hear it.

Your FREDERIC.

Vienna, December 1st, 1830.

I was greatly delighted with your letter, my dearests, the first I have received for a month, that is since I parted from you. My appetite increased a hundred per cent. at once.

" The Wild Man "—as the capital Restaurant

where I dine is called—charged a gulden and some kreuzers for an excellently prepared fritter; what more would you wish?

Titus was full of joy too, for he received letters from his family. I thank Celinski for the accompanying note; it vividly recalled the time when I was still among you; it seemed to me as if I were sitting at the piano, and Celinski standing opposite to me, looking at M. Zwyny, who had just offered Linowski a pinch of snuff. Only Materszynski was wanting to complete the group. Has he recovered from the fever yet?

I must say that there are many charming girls in Vienna.

Haslinger received me very kindly, although he would print neither the Sonata, nor the second Variations, but he shall repent this.

I learned, also, from Haslinger that Fräulein Blahetka is in Stuttgart with her parents, and that, perhaps, she will not come back at all this winter.

I have taken lodgings with Titus in one of the principal streets, close to the vegetable market. For three elegant rooms on the third floor, we pay fifty gulden a month, which is considered cheap here. An English Admiral is occupying them at present, but he leaves to-day. Admiral! And I am admired.* So the house is a desirable one, especially as the

---

* N.B.—Do not show this letter lest I may be thought vain. (Chopin's own observation.)

mistress, a handsome, widowed baroness, still young, has been—as she says—for some time in Poland, and heard of me in Warsaw. She knew the family Skarzynski had moved in good society, and asked Titus if he did not know a beautiful young lady of the name of Rembielinska.

The presence of this charming and intelligent lady makes the apartments all the more agreeable, for she likes Poles, and being a Prussian she regards the Austrians with no great favour.

As soon as we go in Graff, the pianoforte-maker, will send us an instrument. When I went to see my friend Wurfel, he began to talk immediately about arrangements for a concert. He is a remaikable man ; although too ill to go out he gives lessons at his house. He spits blood, which has weakened him very much, and yet he talks of a concert. The poor sufferer told me that the newspapers here wrote enthusiastically about my F minor Concerto, which I had not the remotest expectation of. So I shall give a concert, but when, where, how and what, I do not in the least know.

The change of air has given me a swollen nose, which hindered me from presenting myself at the Prussian Ambassador's hotel, or at Countess Rzeiouska's, the *rendezvous* of all the "haute voleé." This lady lives next to Hussarzewski's, where, in spite of my nose, I have already been two or three times. He is of the same opinion as Wurfel, who advised me to play without honorarium. Dr.

Malfatti * welcomed me as warmly as if I had been a relation. When he read my name on my visiting card, he hastened to me, embraced me, and said, that Herr Wladislaw Ostrowski had written to him about me, and that if he could be of any service he was ready to do anything for me. He said, besides, that he would present me to Madame Tatzszczew, the Russian Ambassador's wife, and would manage the necessary introductions ; the Court was unfortunately in mourning fo. the King of Naples, but he would do what was possible. He also promised to introduce me to Baron Dunoi, director of the Musical Society here, who would probably be most useful to me.

Elsner's letter of recommendation to Herr Mittag procured me another equally agreeable acquaintance, who took a lively interest in me, and seems to be a person of influence.

I have been to see Czerny, who was as polite as ever, and asked, " Have you been studying diligently ? " He has arranged another Oyerture for eight pianos and sixteen players, and seems very happy about it.

Except Czerny, I have seen none of the pianists this time. I have been twice to Frau Weyberheim, Frau Wolf's sister. I am invited to the *soirée* there to-morrow, " en petit cercle des amateurs." I shall

---

* Malfatti, royal physician in ordinary, and a very famous doctor in his time.

pay a visit afterwards to Countess Rosalie Rzewuska, who receives between nine and ten. Hussarzewski has informed her that I am coming; I shall meet the celebrated Frau Cibini,* for whom Moscheles wrote a duet sonata.

Yesterday I went with my letters to Stametz's counting-house, and was received just as if I had come for money. He handed me a paper, which notified that I was to go to the police with my card of permission to stay, and—basta. But perhaps it will be different bye and bye.

I was also at Banker Geymüller's yesterday, where Titus has to receive his 6,000 Polish gulden. When he had read my name Herr Geymüller, without taking any further notice of the letter, said, it was very agreeable to him to become acquainted with an artist of such distinction as myself; but he could not advise me to give a concert here, as there were very many good pianists in the city, and a great reputation was requisite to make money. Finally, he remarked, " I cannot help you in any way, the times are too bad."

I listened with big eyes to this edifying discourse,

---

* Fraulein Cibini was a daughter of Leopold Kozeluck, who, after Mozart's death, became Royal Court Composer. She herself was an accomplished pianist, afterwards lady-in-waiting to the Empress Anna Maria. She nursed the Emperor Ferdinand in his severe illness, and died at the Hradschin, in 1860, highly esteemed as a faithful servant by the Imperial pair.

and when it was over I replied, that I was not at
all sure whether it would pay to make a public
appearance, for I had not yet called upon any
influential people, not even on the Russian Ambassador, to whom I had a letter from the Grand
Prince Constantine.

At that, Herr Geymüller suddenly changed his
tactics; but I took my leave, regretting that I had
robbed him of his precious time, and thought to
myself, " Wait you . . . . Jew."

I have not been to the band-master, Lachner, yet,
as I have not room enough to receive return visits.

We went from the " City of London," where we
had a long bill to pay, to the " Golden Lamb," in
Leopold Street, where we are still, hoping that the
Englishman will quit the Baroness's rooms to-day.
" As soon as we are in our own house," says Titus,
who always tries to make me assume the position
of the haughty patron, " we will introduce an
aristocratic *ton*.   Then," he continued, " we will
receive, have music, and arrange for concerts—but
not gratuitous ones."

I have not yet visited Madame Raayek, Frau von
Elkau, Rothschild, the Vogts, and various other
interesting people.   To-day I am going to the
Embassy, where I hope to see Baron Meindorf,
whom I shall ask for first, on Hussarzewski's
advice, for Baron Meindorf will tell me when I
can best present myself to Herr Tatyszezew.

I have not touched the money which I had from

the banker the day before yesterday. I mean to be very careful of it. I am sorry, my dear parents, but I must ask you to send me something more at the end of the month for the journey to Italy, in case my concerts turn out badly. The theatre is my heaviest expense; but this I regret the less as Fraulein Heinefetter * and Herr Wildt † sing nearly every evening, and are excellent beyond all description. This week I have heard three entirely new operas: " Fra Diavolo " yesterday, three days ago " Titus," and to-day " William Tell." I certainly prefer " The Mutes of Portici " to " Fra Diavolo."

I do not envy Orlowski ‡ because he accompanies Lafont. Will the time come when Lafont shall accompany me? Does the question seem presumptuous? But if God wills it may come to pass.

Nidecki thinks of staying here the whole winter.

---

* Sabine Heinefetter, the most famous and distinguished of the three sisters, who all excelled as great singers; in Milan, even among Italians, she shone as a star of the first magnitude. Circumstances obliged her to leave the stage while still in full possession of her powers.

† Franz Wildt, the most celebrated, and in truth the best tenor singer the German opera possessed from 1820 to 1845. His voice and training were alike first-rate.

‡ Anton Orlowski, a fellow-student of Chopin's, a talented musician, afterwards chapel-master at Rouen. Born in Warsaw 1811, died 1861.

All this week I have done nothing but take care of my nose, go to the opera and to Graff's. I play every afternoon to get my stiff fingers into working order. I do not know how this week has flown. I have, as yet, taken no definite steps towards a concert. *A propos* of that, do you advise me to play the F minor or E minor concerto? Würfel thinks my F minor concerto more beautiful than Hummel's in A flat major, which has just been published by Haslinger. Herr Haslinger is shrewd, trying in a cautious, subtle way, to induce me to let him have my compositions gratis. Klengel was surprised that he gave me nothing for the variations. Perhaps Haslinger thinks that if he treats my works as *bagatelles*, I shall be only too glad to get them printed; but the time for gratuitous work is over with me; now it is, pay *bestie*.

Graff advised me to choose the States Deputies Hall, where the " Spirituel" concerts are given, as the nicest and best place for my concert. But I must first obtain the permission of Count Dietrichstein, which, indeed, will not be difficult through Malfatti.

I am as strong as a lion, and they say I am stouter. Altogether I am doing well, and I hope, through God, who sent Malfatti to be a help to me—oh, splendid Malfatti—that I shall do still better.

CHAPTER X.

THE INSURRECTION IN WARSAW, AND ITS DISASTROUS EFFECT ON CHOPIN'S SOJOURN IN VIENNA.

THE tyrannical rule and the capricious and despotic temper of the Grand Prince Constantine, which the nation had borne with indescribable patience and meekness for fifteen years, at length led to a revolution. The Constitution framed for Poland at the Vienna Congress was regarded in St. Petersburg and Moscow as the work of an encroaching Western Liberalism, and as a revolutionary form of government which threatened to shake the stability of the Russian monarchy. It was, therefore, the constant aim of statesmen on the Neva to circumscribe this hateful Constitution, to make it as far as possible a dead letter, and, finally, to oppress Poland to the uttermost. For the accomplishment of these ends, the advisers of the Czar conceived the idea of sending his brother, the Grand Prince Constantine Pawlowicz, to Warsaw, as plenipotentiary and military governor.

In St. Petersburg, the character of this cruel, coarse man had caused the Emperor numberless embarassments; for the higher State functionaries found him unbearable.

With the title of commander-in-chief of the whole Polish army, Prince Constantine received unlimited power of life and death over the soldiers. He had, at the same time, full authority over all the officials of the kingdom; practically, the Constitution ceased to exist; as early as the year 1819, the freedom of the press had been withdrawn, and a strict censorship established.

When the appointed time arrived, the Diet was not convoked, and faithful patriots who dared to express their opinions were imprisoned. The country swarmed with spies, whose business was to persecute and punish those who showed the least sign of a desire for freedom. Not only the actions, but the half-whispered words, and even the thoughts of the people were betrayed to the Government. Especial severity was exercised towards the young, whom for their natural love of liberty and resistance to despotism the Grand Prince hated with all his heart.

To enforce obedience, the most harsh and unjust means were employed, which could not but embitter the people. The long-cherished wish of Constantine was that the Polish youth should wear a uriform, be enlisted in the army, and thus become the obedient tools of his tyranny. Every young man who devoted himself to science, literature, or the fine arts, instead of entering the army, was, in his eyes, as also in those of the ever vigilant police, either a foolish fanatic, or dangerous to the State. From such proceedings a revolution could not fail, sooner or later, to ensue.

Inflamed by the example of the July revolution in Paris, the Polish youth, whom Constantine hated so intensely, instigated the insurrection of November 29th, 1830. The army and the whole nation followed the revolutionary banners, for all classes were equally incensed against the tyrannical government of the Grand Prince.

At the first news of disquietude in Poland, Titus Woyciechowski at once left Vienna to enter the army. Frederic wished to do the same, as he thought that in such circumstances he could not endure to be so far from his family and friends, and he was only prevented from doing so by the entreaties of his parents, who knew that their son's health was not fit for the hardships of war. Chopin's family were naturally undesirous that he should cut short the artistic career on which he had just entered at so much cost, and in which he had already achieved good success. But his anxiety about his parents and sisters was so great that he followed his friend by the extra post, and had he overtaken him, he would certainly have gone back to Warsaw. Returned to Vienna, Chopin yielded to his father's will, and resumed the idea of giving a concert.

This, however, was not so speedily arranged. The interest of the Viennese musicians had waxed somewhat faint, and he had no benevolent or influential friends among the newly-arrived artists. When he played gratuitously help was readily forthcoming; but the case was altered now, and Frederic saw himself neglected. It is not impossible, in the time of Metternich, that people kept aloof from Poles from motives of prudence; and the energy necessary for overcoming all these obstacles failed Chopin.

Some of his former acquaintances were ill, others had gone away, and the rest were afraid that the agreeable, educated, and highly-gifted artist might settle in Vienna, and thus become a dangerous rival. Many even were displeased at his success in the drawing rooms. The rapid succession of military events in Poland frightened most of his patrons from serving him, while his own mind was more occupied with politics than music.

Several of Frederic's letters, written in a spirit of patriotic enthusiasm, were destroyed by his parents, in case they should fall into the hands of the Russian Government, which had even instituted domiciliary visits. In consequence of the war, much that he wrote never reached Warsaw at all. The sad condition of his country made a deep and lasting impression on the mind of the young artist, so sensitive alike to happiness and sorrow. The gay, buoyant tone of his letters, which had formerly so delighted their recipients, changed to a certain discontent and sadness; even his pleasant wit, as the reader will see by the following correspondence, was frequently turned into bitter sarcasm.

Vienna,

Wednesday before Christmas-day.

(I have no almanack at hand, so do not know the day.)

DEAREST PARENTS AND SISTERS,

It was seven weeks, yesterday, since I left you. What for? But it is so, and cannot be helped.

I was invited, yesterday, at the very hour that I was conducted to Wola, to a little dancing party, at the Weiberheim's.. There were several handsome young people there, not old-fashioned looking, that is, not Old Testament-looking.*

I was pressed to join the Cotillon; so I went round a few times and then returned home. The hostess and her amiable daughters had asked several musical people, but I was not in a humour for playing the piano.

Herr Likl, who knows Louise, was introduced to me. He is a good, honest German, and thinks me a great man; so I would not destroy his good opinion by playing when I was not in the right mood. I also spoke to Lampi's nephew, who knows

* Viz., not Jewish.

Papa well. He is a handsome, agreeable young man, and paints very well. *A propos* of painting, Hummel and his son were with me yesterday. The latter has now almost finished my portrait. It is so good, one cannot imagine it better. I am sitting in my dressing-gown, with a look of inspiration which I do not know why the artist should have given me. The portrait is in quarto size, drawn in chalk, and looks like a steel engraving. The elder Hummel was exceedingly polite, and introduced me to his old acquaintance, M. Duport, director of the Kärthner-Thor Theatre. The latter, who has been a celebrated dancer, is said to be very stingy; however, he was exceedingly complaisant to me, thinking, perhaps, that I should play gratuitously for him. He makes a mistake there! We had a sort of conference together, but nothing definite was decided on. If Herr Duport offers too little, I shall give my concert in the large Redoubt Hall.

Würfel is better; I met Slawick, an excellent violinist,* at his house last week. He is at the most twenty-six, and pleased me very much. When we left Würfel's he asked me if I were going home, to which I replied in the affirmative. "Come with me instead, to your countrywoman's, Frau Beyer's, said

---

* Joseph Slawick, born in Bohemia in 1806, studied at the Prague Conservatoire, under Pixis, at the expense of Count Wrbna; de died at Pesth in 1833, just as he was about to commence a long artistic tour.

Slawick. I agreed. Now Kraszewski had sent me, the same day, from Dresden, a letter to Frau Beyer, but without any address, and Beyer is a common name in Vienna. So I resolved at once to fetch my letter and go with Slawick; when, lo and behold! I really went to the right Frau Beyer. Her husband is a Pole from Odessa. She declared that she had heard of me, and invited both Slawick and myself to dinner the next day.

After dinner Slawick played, and pleased me immensely, more than any one since Paganini. As my playing was also agreeable to him, we determined to compose a duet together for violin and piano. I had thought of doing so in Warsaw. Slawick is, indeed, a great and talented violinist. When I become acquainted with Merk, we shall be able to manage a trio. I hope to meet him soon at Mechetti's.

Czerny was with me at Diabelli's, yesterday; the latter invited me to a *soirée* on Monday next, where I am to meet none but artists. On Sunday there is a *soirée* at Likl's, where the aristocratic musical world assemble, and the Overture for four performers is to be given. On Saturday there is to be a performance of old church music at Kiesewetter's (author of a work on music.)

I am living on the fourth floor; some English people took such a fancy to my abode, that they said they would rent it of me for eighty gulden; a proposal to which I acceded most willingly. My

M

young and agreeable hostess, Frau Baroness of
Lachmanowicz, sister-in-law of Frau von Uszakow,
has just as roomy apartments on the fourth storey for
twenty gulden, which satisfy me quite well. I know
you will say, " the poor wretch lives in a garret."
But it is not so; there is another floor between me
and the roof, and eighty gulden are not to be despised
either. People visit me notwithstanding; even Count
Hussarzweski took the trouble to mount up. The
street is in an advantageous position for me, in the
midst of the city, close to where I most often want
to go. Artaria is at the left, Mechetti and Haslinger
are at my right, and the Royal Opera Theatre is
behind. Could I have anything more convenient?

I have not yet written to Herr Elsner, but I was
at Czerny's just now. Up till to-day, the Quartett
has not appeared.

Dr. Malfatti scolded me for appearing at Madame
Schaschek's to dinner at four instead of two. I am
to dine with Malfatti again next Saturday, and if I
am late again, Malfatti will—so he threatens—
subject me to a painful operation.

I can imagine dear Papa looking grave over my
frivolity, and want of respect to my elders; but I
will improve. I am proud to say that Malfatti is
really fond of me. Nidecki comes to me every day
to play. If my concerto for two pianos succeeds to
my satisfaction, we are going to play it together in
public, but I shall play alone first.

Haslinger is always pleasant, but does not say

a word about publishing. Shall I go shortly to
Italy, or shall I wait?* Dearest Papa, please tell
me what are your and dear Mamma's wishes.

I daresay Mamma is glad I did not return to
Warsaw, but how I should like to be there!
Embrace dear Titus for me, and beg him to write
me a few words.

I know you believe in my affection and deep
attachment; but you can scarcely imagine what a
very great delight your letters are to me. Why is
not the post quicker? You will think it natural that
I should be very anxious about you, and impatiently
await news of you.

I have made a very agreeable acquaintance, a
young man of the name of Leibenfrost; he is a
friend of Kessler's. We meet frequently, and when
I am not invited out we dine together in the city.
He knows Vienna perfectly, and will be sure to take
me to see whatever is worth seeing. For instance,
yesterday, we had a splendid walk to the fortifica-
tions; Dukes, Princes, Counts, in a word, all the
aristocracy of Vienna were assembled there. I met
Slawick, and we agreed to choose a Beethoven theme
for our Variations.

For some reasons I am very glad that I am here,
but for others! . . . . .

I am very comfortable in my room; there is a
roof opposite, and the people walking below look like

---

* A reference, perhaps, to the disturbances then prevailing
in the Peninsular.

dwarfs. I am most happy, when I have played to my heart's content on Graff's magnificent instrument. Now I am going to sleep with your letters in my hand; then I shall dream only of you.

The Mazurka was danced, yesterday, at Beyer's. Slawick fell down with his partner, an old Countess with a coarse face and a large nose, who daintily held her dress in the old-fashioned way, by the tips of her fingers, her head resting on the flap of his coat. But all respect to the couple, and to the lady in particular, who is sensible and entertaining and knows the *usage du monde*.

Among the most popular of the numerous amusements of Vienna are the Garden Concerts, where Launer and Strauss play waltzes while the public sup. After every waltz the musicians receive a boisterous bravo. If an *ad libitum* is played, introducing favourite operatic melodies, songs, and dances, the enthusiasm of the Viennese knows no bounds.

I wanted to send you with this my last Waltz, but the post goes, and I have no time to write it out, so must wait till another opportunity. The Mazurkas, too, I must get copied first; but they are not for dancing.

I do not like to say goodbye already; I would gladly write more. If you should see Fontana tell him that he shall soon have a letter from me. Matuszynski will have a long epistle either to-day or by the next post.

Farewell, my dearests,

Your FREDERIC.

To John Matuszynski.

Vienna,

Sunday, Christmas Morning.

This time last year I was in the Bernhardine church, to-day I am sitting in my dressing gown, quite alone ; I kiss my sweet ring and write.*

Dear Hanschen,

I have just come from hearing the famous violinist, Slawick, who is second only to Paganini. He takes sixty-nine staccato notes at one stroke of the bow ! It is almost incredible ! When I heard him I wanted to rush home and sketch out some variations for piano and violin on an Adagio by Beethoven ; but a glance at the post office, which I always pass (that I may ask for letters from home), diverted my desires.

The tears which this heavenly theme brought to my eyes have moistened your letter. I long, unspeakably, for a word from you ; you know why.

How any news of my angel of peace always delights me !

How gladly would I touch the strings which should awaken not only stormy feelings, but the songs whose half echoes still haunt the shores of the

---

* Fraulein Constantia Gladkowska was in the habit of going to the Bernhardine Church, which was close to the Conservatoire.

Danube—songs sung by the warriors of King John Sobieski.

You advised me to choose a poet. But you know that I am an indecisive being, and only once in my life made a good choice.

I would not willingly be a burden to my father; were I not afraid of that, I should immediately return to Warsaw. I am often in such a mood that I curse the moment in which I left my beloved home. You will, I am sure, understand my condition, and that since Titus went away too much has fallen suddenly upon me. The numerous dinners, *soirées*, concerts, and balls I am obliged to attend only weary me. I am melancholy. I feel so lonely and deserted here, yet I cannot live as I like. I have to dress, and look cheerful in drawing rooms; but when I am in my room again, I talk to my piano, to whom, as my best friend in Vienna, I pour out all my sorrows. There is not a soul I can unreservedly confide in, and yet I have to treat everyone as a friend. Plenty of people seem, indeed, to like me, take my portrait, and seek after my company, but they do not make up for you. I have lost my peace of mind, and only feel happy when I can read your letters, think of the monument of King Sigismund,* or look at my precious ring.

Pray forgive me, dear Hänschen, for writing so

---

* The Conservatoire, where Constantia boarded, was near the statue of King Sigismund.

complainingly, but my heart feels lighter when I can thus talk to you, and I have always told you everything that concerned myself. Did you receive a short letter from me the day before yesterday? Perhaps my scribbling is not of much consequence to you as you are at home, but I read your letters again and again.

Dr. Freyer, having learnt from Schuch that I was in Vienna, has been to see me two or three times. He gave me a great deal of interesting news, and was very pleased with your letters, which I read to him up to a certain passage, which passage made me feel very sad. Does she really look so changed? Do you think she was ill? She is of such a sensitive nature that this is not at all unlikely. But, perhaps, it was only your imagination, or she had been frightened by something. God forbid that she should suffer anything on my account! Comfort her, and assure her that as long as my heart beats I shall not cease to adore her. Tell her that, after my death, my ashes shall be spread beneath her feet. But this is not half what you might say to her on my behalf. I would write to her myself, and, indeed, should have done so long ago, to escape the torments I endure, but if my letter chanced to fall into other hands, might it not injure her reputation? So you must be the interpreter of my thoughts; speak for me, "et j'en conviendrai." These words of yours flashed through me like lightning, when I read your letter. A

Viennese, who happened to be walking with me at the time, seized me by the arm, and could scarcely hold me in. He could not make out what had come to me. I could have embraced and kissed all the passers by, for your first letter had made my heart feel lighter than it had been for many a day.

I am sure I must be wearying you, my dear friend, but it is difficult for me to hide from you anything that touches my heart. The day before yesterday I dined with Frau Beyer, who is also called Constantia. I enjoy visiting her very much, because she bears a name so unspeakably dear to me; I even rejoice if one of her pocket-handkerchiefs or serviettes marked "Constantia" falls into my hands. Slawick is a friend of hers, and I often go to her house with him.

Yesterday, as on Christmas Eve, we played in the fore and afternoon. The weather was spring-like. As I was returning in the evening from the Baroness's circle, I walked slowly into St. Stephen's. I was alone, for Slawick was obliged to go to the Imperial Chapel. The church was empty, and, to get the full effect of the lofty and imposing edifice, I leant against a pillar in the darkest corner. The vastness and splendour of the arching are indescribable: one must see St. Stephen's for one's self. The profoundest silence, broken only by the resounding steps of the vergers coming to light the tapers, reigned around.

Before and behind me, indeed everywhere but

overhead, were graves, and I felt my loneliness and desertion as I never had before. When the lights had burned up, and the cathedral began to fill, I muffled myself in my cloak (you know how I used to go about in the Cracow suburb), and hastened off to the Mass at the Imperial Chapel. Amid a merry crowd, I threaded my way to the palace, where I heard some sleepy musicians play three movements of a mass. I returned home at one o'clock in the morning, and went to bed to dream of you, of her, and of my dear children.*

Next morning I was awakened by an invitation to dinner from Frau Elkan, a Polish lady, and the wife of a well-known wealthy banker. The first thing I did that day was to play some melancholy fantasias, and, after receiving calls from Nidecki, Liebenfrost, and Steinkeller, I went to dine with Malfatti. This excellent man thinks of everything; he even goes so far as to provide dishes cooked in Polish fashion.

Wildt, the famous tenor, came after dinner. I accompanied him, from memory, in an air from "Otello," which he sang admirably. Wildt and Fräulein Heinefetter are the stars of the Royal opera; the other singers are not so good as one would expect. But a voice like Heinefetter's is very rare; her intonation also is always pure, her colouring refined, and, indeed, her singing altogether

---

* Chopin often called his sisters his children.

faultless; but she is cold; I nearly got my nose
frozen in the pit. She looks particularly handsome
as a man. I liked her better in "Otello" than in
"Barbiere," in which she represented the con-
summate coquette, instead of the lively witty girl.
As Sextus in "Titus" she was exceedingly brilliant.
In a few days she will appear in "Der Diebische
Elster," which I am curious to see. Fräulein
Wolkow pleased me better as Rosine in the
"Barbiere," but she certainly has not the voice
of Heinefetter. I wished I had heard Pasta.

You know that I have letters from the Saxon
court to the Viceroy of Milan, but what had I best
do? My parents leave me to follow my own wishes,
but I would rather they had given me directions.
Shall I go to Paris? Friends here advise me to
stay in Vienna. Or shall I go home, or stay here
and kill myself? Advise me what to do. Please
ask a certain person in Warsaw, who has always
had great influence over me. Tell me her opinion,
and I will act upon it.

Let me hear again before you go to the war.
Address, Poste Restante, Vienna. Do go and see
my dear parents and Constantia; and, as long as
you are in Warsaw, please pay frequent visits to my
sisters that they way think you are coming to see
me, and I am in the next room; sit with them
that they may fancy it is me; in a word, take my
place at home.

I am not thinking any more of concert-giving

just now. Aloys Schmitt, the pianist from Frank-
fort-on-the-Maine, whose studies are so famous, is
here at present. He is something over forty years
of age. I have made his acquaintance, and he
promised to come and see me. He intends giving
a concert, and it must be admitted that he is a
clever musician. On musical matters we shall, I
think, soon understand one another.

Thalberg is also here, and playing famously, but
he is not the man for me. He is younger than I am,
very popular with the ladies, makes *pot-pourris* on the
"Mutes," plays *forte* and *piano* with the pedals, but
not with his hands, takes tenths as I do octaves, and
wears diamond studs. He does not at all admire
Moscheles; so it is not surprising that the *tutti* were
the only part of my concerto that pleased him. He,
too, writes concertos.

I finish this letter three days after I began it, and
have read through my stupid scribble again. Pray
excuse having to pay the postage, dear Hanschen.
When dining to-day at the Italian restaurant, I
heard some one say, "God made a mistake in
creating Poland." Is it any wonder that my feelings
are more than I can express ? Somebody else said,
"There is nothing to be got out of Poland," so you
ought not to expect anything new from me who
am a Pole.

There is a Frenchman here who makes all kinds
of sausages, and for a month past crowds have
gathered round his attractive shop, for there is

something new in it every day. Some people imagine that they are beholding the remains of the French Revolution, and look compassionately at the sausages and hams, which hang up like pictures, or they are indignant at the revolutionary French-man being allowed to open a meat shop, as there were quite enough pigs in his own country. He is the talk of Vienna, and there is a general dread that if there should be a disturbance the French will be at the bottom of it.

I must close, for the time is quite up. Embrace all my dear friends for me, and be assured that I shall not leave off loving you till I have ceased to love my parents, my sisters, and her. My dearest, do write me a few lines soon. You can show this to her if you like. I am going to Malfatti's again to-day, but to the post first. My parents do not know of my writing to you. You can tell them, only don't show them the letter.

I do not know how to part from my sweet Hänschen. Depart, you wretch! If W—— loves you as warmly as I do, so would Con . . . . . No, I cannot even write the name, my hand is too unworthy. Oh! I should tear my hair out if I thought she forgot me: I feel a regular Othello to-day. I was about to fold and seal the letter without an envelope, forgetting that it was going where everybody reads Polish. As I have a little space left, I will describe my life here.

I am living on the fourth floor in a handsome

street, but I have to be on the alert if I want to see what passes. When I come home you will see the room in my new album, young Hummel having kindly made me a drawing of it. It is spacious, and has five windows, to which the bed stands opposite. My wonderful piano stands on the right, the sofa on the left, a looking-glass between the windows, a large handsome round mahogany table in the middle of the room; the floor is waxed. Don't be alarmed! . . . .

"The gentleman does not receive in the afternoon," so I can be in your midst in thought. The intolerably stupid servant wakes me early; I rise, take my coffee, which is often cold, because I forget my breakfast over my music. My German teacher appears punctually at 9 o'clock; then I generally write, Hummel comes to work at my portrait, and Nidecki to study my Concerto. I keep on my comfortable dressing-gown till 12 o'clock, at which hour Dr. Leibenfrost, a lawyer here, comes in to see me. Weather permitting, I walk with him on the Glacis, then we dine at the " Zum Bömischen Kochin," the *rendezvous* of the students from the Academy, and afterwards, according to the custom here, we go to one of the best coffee-houses. Then I make calls, returning home at dusk, when I throw myself into evening dress, and go to a *soirée*. About 11 or 12 o'clock (never later) I come home, play, laugh, read, and then go to bed and dream of you.

My portrait—which is a secret between you and me—is very good. If you think she would like it I could send it through Schuch, who will probably leave here with Freyer, about the 15th of next month. I began to write this letter quite clearly, but I have finished it in such a way that you will have some trouble in reading it. Embrace my college friends, and, if possible, get them to write to me. Kindest love to Elsner.

To the same.

Vienna,
New Year's Day, 1831.

DEAREST HEART,

Now you have what you wanted. Did you receive the letter, and deliver any of it? I still regret what I have done. I *was* full of sweet hopes, and *now* I am tormented with doubt and anxiety. Perhaps she scorns me, or laughs at me! Perhaps— oh, does she love me? asks my throbbing heart. You good-for-nothing Esculapius. You were in the theatre with your opera glasses, and did not take your eyes off her! If that is so, confound it. . . . . Do not make light of my confidence, but I only write to you for my own sake; you are not worth the trouble. Now you know all my thoughts. When you are in your room with your old friends Rostowski, Schuch, Freyer, Kyjewski, and Hube, imagine that I am enjoying myself with you, but oh! I feel so strange in writing to you here. It seems as if I were with you, and what I see and hear around me only a dream. The voices to which my ear is unaccustomed seem to me only like the rattling of a carriage, or some other unimportant sound. Only your or Titus's voice could wake me out of my stupor. To-day, life and death are indifferent to me. Say nothing of this to my parents. Tell them that I am in capital spirits, that I want for nothing, am enjoying myself gloriously, and never feel lonely. Tell her the same, if she laughs at me, but if she asks kindly after me, and seems anxious about me, whisper to her not to be uneasy, but say that I am very lonely and unhappy away from her. I am not well, but do not tell my parents. All my friends are asking what ails me; "humour," I sometimes say, but you know what is really the matter.

At the end of next month I shall go to Paris, if things remain quiet there. There is no lack of amusements here, but I very seldom care to participate in them. Merk, the first violinist in Vienna, has promised me a visit. This is the first of January. Oh, what a sad beginning of the year for me! I love you dearly. Write as soon as possible. Is she at Radom? Have you built forts? My poor parents! How are my friends? I would die for you, for any of you. Why am I condemned to stay here, lonely and forsaken? You who are together, can comfort one another in these fearful times. Your flute will have enough to mourn over? How my piano will weep itself out!

You write that you a. g..ng to take ..e field with your regiment; how wi.. you forward the letter? Do not send it by a messenger; be careful! My parents might—they might misunderstand.

Once more I embrace you. You are going to the war; come back a colonel. May all go well! Why can I not at least be your drummer? Excuse this rambling letter, for I feel quite dazed.

Your faithful

FREDERIC.*

---

* This letter, written on two loose sheets, was found enclosed in one to his parents, which had no envelope, and was only slightly sealed. Frederic had written under the direction these words to his sisters, "You are requested not to break the seal, and not to be inquisitive, like old women."

LaVergne, TN USA
20 December 2010
209464LV00003B/16/P

9 781172 078363